Effective Monitoring and Alerting

Slawek Ligus

O'REILLY®

Beijing · Cambridge · Farnham · Köln · Sebastopol · Tokyo

Effective Monitoring and Alerting

by Slawek Ligus

Published by O'Reilly Media, Inc., 1005 Gravenstein Highway North, Sebastopol, CA 95472.

O'Reilly books may be purchased for educational, business, or sales promotional use. Online editions are also available for most titles (*http://my.safaribooksonline.com*). For more information, contact our corporate/institutional sales department: 800-998-9938 or *corporate@oreilly.com*.

Editors: Andy Oram and Mike Hendrickson	**Proofreader:** Mary Ellen Smith
Production Editor: Rachel Steely	**Cover Designer:** Karen Montgomery
	Interior Designer: David Futato
	Illustrator: Robert Romano

Revision History for the First Edition:

2012-11-20 First release

See *http://oreilly.com/catalog/errata.csp?isbn=9781449333522* for release details.

ISBN: 978-1-449-33352-2

[LSI]

Table of Contents

Preface

I've been fortunate to get hired into medium-sized operations teams at large technology companies. All ops teams (a customary term for operations teams) share two interesting characteristics: compared to other engineering departments, they work under more pressure, and they attract bad attention much easier than good attention. Digital fire-fighting is the nature of the job. We might get noticed when things go awry and we fix them. If we don't react fast enough, we definitely get noticed. If you know anyone in network operations, ask if that's the way he or she feels about the job—I bet you're going to get an answer along those lines.

Working in ops is all about effectiveness: there is no time for re-engineering. We must get things right the first time and we have to act fast. We go through a lot of reprioritizing and context-switching. There is relatively little room for creativity, at least the kind that doesn't love constraints. All this makes operations a great place to learn and grow.

This book is based on experiences of working in ops. I was extremely lucky to work with some of the smartest people in the industry. I would like this book to be a tribute to all these invisible ops guys who struggle daily to maintain the highest standards of service availability.

In my career, I've stared at all sorts of timeseries plots, a lot of them. At one point it was my full-time job—no kidding. With time, I learned to extract meaning from data point fluctuations just by a brief glance, without having to study their origin. It's a funny kind of intuition that system engineers develop in the course of their jobs, and one that probably saves us a lot of time. Some of us are unaware of it, and it's definitely not something we brag about. It is a very useful skill, nevertheless, and in this book I attempt to verbalize it in order to assist you, dear Reader, to absorb it in a more conscious way than I did, possibly saving you weeks or months of getting up to speed.

Some people on my team believed that putting in motion the ideas described here led to a visible paradigm shift. I must agree that in a relatively short period of time, the work caused by our alerting configuration went from mundane to effortless.

This book focuses on monitoring and alerting in the context of distributed information systems, but I'm hoping that the principles presented here will also be applicable to timeseries and datasets generated by all sorts of complex systems. The book does not focus on any particular software package. Rather, it attempts to extract and summarize regularities that system engineers come across in their daily work. You won't find many long code listings here, but you'll definitely find ideas: ones that I hope you'll be able to relate to and apply either at work or in a research project.

Enjoy!

Who Should Read This Book

The main audience of this book are system operators, those who fight the daily battle of delivering the best performance at lowest cost as well as those who use monitoring as a means and not an end. Read it if you work extensively with monitoring and plan alerting configurations. If keeping high availability and continuity of service is your job, read on. If monitoring and alerting bring up unpleasant associations, that's an even more valid reason to read the book. If you're trying to quantify the effectiveness of your alerting configurations, the book might have good answers.

Administrators who are setting up a monitoring or alerting configuration with a potential to grow big might also find the book useful. The ideas presented here have been tested on large alerting configurations with a high degree of success. By "large," I mean thousands of monitors and hundreds of alarms. The book should help you replicate this setup in your environment.

Conventions Used in This Book

The following typographical conventions are used in this book:

Italic
> Indicates new terms, URLs, email addresses, filenames, and file extensions.

`Constant width`
> Used for program listings, as well as within paragraphs to refer to program elements such as variable or function names, databases, data types, environment variables, statements, and keywords.

`Constant width bold`
> Shows commands or other text that should be typed literally by the user.

Constant width italic
> Shows text that should be replaced with user-supplied values or by values determined by context.

This icon signifies a tip, suggestion, or general note.

This icon indicates a warning or caution.

Using Code Examples

This book is here to help you get your job done. In general, if this book includes code examples, you may use the code in your programs and documentation. You do not need to contact us for permission unless you're reproducing a significant portion of the code. For example, writing a program that uses several chunks of code from this book does not require permission. Selling or distributing a CD-ROM of examples from O'Reilly books does require permission. Answering a question by citing this book and quoting example code does not require permission. Incorporating a significant amount of example code from this book into your product's documentation does require permission.

We appreciate, but do not require, attribution. An attribution usually includes the title, author, publisher, and ISBN. For example: "*Effective Monitoring and Alerting* by Slawek Ligus (O'Reilly). Copyright 2013 Slawek Ligus, 978-1-449-33352-2."

If you feel your use of code examples falls outside fair use or the permission given above, feel free to contact us at *permissions@oreilly.com*.

Safari® Books Online

Safari Safari Books Online (*www.safaribooksonline.com*) is an on-demand
Books Online digital library that delivers expert content in both book and video
form from the world's leading authors in technology and business.

Technology professionals, software developers, web designers, and business and creative professionals use Safari Books Online as their primary resource for research, problem solving, learning, and certification training.

Safari Books Online offers a range of product mixes and pricing programs for organizations, government agencies, and individuals. Subscribers have access to thousands of books, training videos, and prepublication manuscripts in one fully searchable database from publishers like O'Reilly Media, Prentice Hall Professional, Addison-Wesley

Professional, Microsoft Press, Sams, Que, Peachpit Press, Focal Press, Cisco Press, John Wiley & Sons, Syngress, Morgan Kaufmann, IBM Redbooks, Packt, Adobe Press, FT Press, Apress, Manning, New Riders, McGraw-Hill, Jones & Bartlett, Course Technology, and dozens more. For more information about Safari Books Online, please visit us online.

How to Contact Us

Please address comments and questions concerning this book to the publisher:

O'Reilly Media, Inc.
1005 Gravenstein Highway North
Sebastopol, CA 95472
800-998-9938 (in the United States or Canada)
707-829-0515 (international or local)
707-829-0104 (fax)

We have a web page for this book, where we list errata, examples, and any additional information. You can access this page at *http://oreil.ly/Monitoring_and_Alerting*.

The author has set up a small blog for this book. It can be accessed at *http://effectivemo nitoring.info/*.

To comment or ask technical questions about this book, send email to *bookques tions@oreilly.com*.

For more information about our books, courses, conferences, and news, see our website at *http://www.oreilly.com*.

Find us on Facebook: *http://facebook.com/oreilly*

Follow us on Twitter: *http://twitter.com/oreillymedia*

Watch us on YouTube: *http://www.youtube.com/oreillymedia*

Acknowledgements

I'd like to start by saying thanks to my grandparents, Zuzanna and Marian Osiak, who in 1998 helped me buy my first O'Reilly book, the first edition of *Linux in a Nutshell* by Ellen Siever et al., when at 13 years of age I was on a very limited budget. Specifically, grandma Zuzia persuaded the shop clerk in Katowice, Poland to drop the price by 50% despite bookstore's strict policy of not offering discounts in excess of 20%. Little did we suspect that after fast-forwarding into the future by a decade and a half, I got to work with Ellen's editor, who created the idea of this Linux book.

The person most helpful in the creation of the book was my wonderful partner, Natalia Czachowicz, who assisted me at all stages of the authoring process from coming up with an idea and writing the proposal through to setting up the plan, its execution and finalizing. Natalia acted as my consultant, editor, reviewer, proofreader, marketer and counsellor, and the amount of support she provided is ineffable; Nati, I'm indebted to you for life!

I want to offer my gratitude to Benoît "tsuna" Sigoure, my technical reviewer, whose critical remarks and suggestions greatly added to the value of this book. Special thanks go to Viktor "vic" Trnka who kindly allowed me to instrument the network and systems of MS-Free.NET to use generated data points for illustrations. Last but certainly not least I'd like to give credit to Andy Oram, who patiently edited our way into completion of this work.

I'd also like to take this opportunity to say massive thanks to all my friends and family for enormous support in idea bouncing, spreading the word on social networks, proofreading and for all kind words I received in the process—thank you all, it really meant a lot.

## CHAPTER 1

Introduction

Present-day information systems have became so complex that troubleshooting them effectively necessitates real-time performance, data presented at fine granularity, a thorough understanding of data interpretation, and a pinch of skill. The time when you could trace failure to a few possible causes is long gone. Availability standards in the industry remain high and are pushed ever further. The systems must be equipped with powerful instrumentation, otherwise lack of information will lead to loss of time and—in some cases—loss of revenue.

Monitoring empowers operators to catch complications before they develop into problems, and helps you preserve high availability and deliver high quality of service. It also assists you in making informed decisions about the present and the future, serves as input to automation of infrastructures and, most importantly, is an indispensable learning tool.

Monitoring, Alerting, and What They Can Do for You

Monitoring has become an umbrella term whose meaning strongly depends on the context. Most broadly, it refers to the process of becoming aware of the state of a system. This is done in two ways, proactive and reactive. The former involves watching visual indicators, such as timeseries and dashboards, and is sometimes what administrators mean by *monitoring*. The latter involves automated ways to deliver notifications to operators in order to bring to their attention a grave change in system's state; this is usually referred to as *alerting*.

But the ambiguity doesn't end there. Look around on forums and mailing lists and you'll realize that some people use the term *monitoring* to refer to the process of measurement, which might not necessarily involve any human interaction. I'm sure my definitions here are not exhaustive. The point is that, when you read about monitoring, it is useful to discern as early as possible what process the writer is actually talking about.

Some goals of monitoring are more obvious than others. To demonstrate its full potential, let me point out the most common use cases, which are connected to overseeing data flow and the process of change in your system.

Defining Monitoring and Alerting

Because there are many ways to view these activities, I'll provide some more formal definitions that may help you put each of the activities in this book in context.

Monitoring is the process of maintaining surveillance over the existence and magnitude of state change and data flow in a system. Monitoring aims to identify faults and assist in their subsequent elimination. The techniques used in monitoring of information systems intersect the fields of real-time processing, statistics, and data analysis. A set of software components used for data collection, their processing, and presentation is called a *monitoring system*.

Alerting is the capability of a monitoring system to detect and notify the operators about meaningful events that denote a grave change of state. The notification is referred to as an *alert* and is a simple message that may take multiple forms: email, SMS, instant message (IM), or a phone call. The alert is passed on to the appropriate recipient, that is, a party responsible for dealing with the event. The alert is often logged in the form of a ticket in an *Issue Tracking System* (ITS), also referred to simply as ticketing system.

Early Problem Detection

Speedy detection of threatening issues is by far the most important objective of monitoring and is the function of the alerting part of the system. The difficulty consists of pursuing two conflicting goals: speed and accuracy. I want to know when something is not right and I want to know about it fast. I do not, however, want to get alarmed because of temporary blips and transient issues of negligible impact. Behind every reasonable threshold value lurks a risk for potentially disastrous issues slipping under the radar. This is precisely why setting up alarms manually is very hard and speculating about the right threshold levels in meetings can be exhausting, frustrating, and unproductive. The goal of effective alerting is to minimize the hazards.

Availability

In the business of availability, *downtime* is a dreaded term. It happens when the system is subject to full *loss of availability*. Availability loss can also be partial, or unavailable only for a portion of users. The key is early detection and prevention in busy production environments.

Downtime usually translates directly to losses in revenue. A complete monitoring setup that allows for timely identification of issues proves indispensable. Ideally, monitoring tools should enable operators to drill down from a high-level overview into the fine levels of detail, granular enough to point at specifics used in analysis and identification of a *root cause*.

The root cause establishes the real reason (and its many possible factors) behind the fault. The subsequent corrective action builds upon the findings from root cause analysis and is carried out to prevent future occurrences of the problem. Fixing the most superficial problem only (or *proximate cause*) guarantees recurrence of the same faults in the long run.

Performance

Paying close attention to anomalous behavior in the system help to detect resource saturation and rare defects. A number of faults get by Quality Assurance (QA), are hard to account for, and are likely to surface only after long hours of regression testing. A peculiar group of rare bugs emerge exclusively at large scale when exposed to extremely heavy system load. Although hard to isolate in test environments, they are consistently reproducible in production. And once they are located through scrupulous monitoring, they are easier to identify and eliminate.

Decision Making

Operators develop a strong intuition about shifts in utilization patterns. The ability to discern anomalies from visual plots is a big part of their job knowledge. Sometimes operators must make decisions quickly, and in critical situations, knowing your system well can reduce blunders and improve your chances for successful mitigation. Other times, intuition leads to unfounded assumptions and acting on them may lead to catastrophic outcomes. Comprehensive monitoring helps you verify wild guesses and gut feelings.

Baselining

Monitoring provides an immediate insight into a system's current state. This data often takes quantitative form and, when recorded on timeseries, become a rich source of information for baselining.

Establishing standard performance levels is an important part of your job. It finds application in capacity planning, leads to formulation of data-backed *Service-Level Agreements* (SLAs) and, where inconsistencies are detected, can be a starting point for in-depth performance analysis.

Predictions

In the context of monitoring, a *prediction* is a quantitative forecast containing a degree of uncertainty about future levels of resources or phenomena leading to their utilization. Monitoring traffic and usage patterns over time serves as a source of information for decision support. It can help you predict what normal traffic levels are during peaks and troughs, holidays, and key periods such as major global sporting events. When the usage patterns trend outside the projected limits, there probably is a good reason for it, even if this reason is not directly dependent on the system's operation. For instance, traffic patterns that drop below 20% of the expected values for an extended period might stem from a portion of customers experiencing difficulties with their ISPs. Some Internet giants are able to conclusively narrow down the source of external failure and proactively help ISPs identify and mitigate against faults.

On top of predicting future workload, close interaction with monitoring may help predict business trends. Customers may have different needs at different times of the year. The ability to predict demands and then match them based on seasonality translates directly into revenue gains.

Automation

Metrics are a source of quantitative information, and the evaluation of an alarm state results in a boolean yes-no answer to the simple question: is the monitored value within expected limits? This has important implications for the automation of processes, especially those involving admission control, pause of operation, and estimations based on real-time data.

Admission Control

Bursts of input may saturate a system's capacity and it may have to drop some traffic. In order to prevent uniformly bad experience for all users an attempt is made to reject a portion of inputs. This is commonly known as *admission control* and its objective is to defend against thrashing that severely denigrates performance.

Some implementations of admission control are known as the Big Red Button (BRB), as they require a human engineer to intervene and press it. Deciding when to stop admission is inherently inefficient: such decisions are usually made too late, they often require an approval or sign-off, and there is always the danger of someone forgetting to toggle the button back to the unpressed state when the situation is back under control.

Consider the potential of using inputs from monitoring for admission control. Monitoring-enabled mechanisms go into effect immediately when the problems are first detected, allowing for gradual and local degradation before sudden and global disasters. When the problem subsides, the protecting mechanism stops without the need for human supervision.

Autonomic Computing

Monitoring's feedback loop is also central to the idea of *Autonomic Computing* (AC), an architecture in which the system is capable of regulating itself and thus enabling self-management and self-healing. AC was inspired by the operation of the human central nervous system. It draws an analogy between it and a complex, distributed information system. Unconscious processes, such as the control over the rate of breath, do not require human effort. The goal of AC is to minimize the need for human intervention in a similar way, by replacing it with self-regulation. Comprehensive monitoring can provide an effective means to achieve this end.

Monitoring and Alerting in a Nutshell

Having discussed what these processes are for, let's move on to how they're done. Monitoring is a continuous process, a series of steps carried out in a loop. This section outlines its workings and introduces monitoring's fundamental building blocks.

Metrics and Timeseries

Watching and evaluating *timeseries*, chronologically ordered lists of data points, is at the core of both monitoring and alerting.

Monitoring consists of recording and analyzing quantitative inputs, that is, numeric measurements carrying information about current state and its most recent changes. Each data input comes with a number of properties describing it: the origin of the measurement and its attributes such as units and time at which sampling took place.

The inputs along with their properties are stored in the form of *metrics*. A metric is a data structure optimized for storage and retrieval of numeric inputs. The resulting collection of gathered inputs may be interpreted in many different ways based on the values of their assigned properties. Such interpretation allows a tool to evaluate the inputs as a whole as well as at many abstract levels, from coarse to fine granularity.

Data inputs extracted from selected metrics are further agglomerated into groups based on the time the measurement occurred. The groups are assigned to uniform intervals on a time axis, and the total of inputs in each group can be summarized by use of a mathematical transformation, referred to as a *summary statistic*. The mathematical transformation yields one numeric data point for each time interval. The collection of data points, a timeseries, describes some statistical aspect of all inputs from a given time range. The same set of data inputs may be used to generate different data points, depending on the selection of a summary statistic.

Alarms, Alerts, and Monitors

An alarm is a piece of configuration describing a system's change in state, most typically a highly undesirable one, through fluctuations of data points in a timeseries. Alarms are made up of metric monitors and date-time evaluations and may optionally nest other alarms.

An alert is a notification of a potential problem, which can take one or more of the following forms: email, SMS, phone call, or a ticket. An alert is issued by an alarm when the system transitions through some threshold, and this threshold breach is detected by a monitor. Thus, for example, you may configure an alarm to alert you when the system exceeds 80% of CPU utilization for a continuous period of 10 minutes.

A metric monitor is attached to a timeseries and evaluates it against a threshold. The threshold consists of limits (expressed as the number of data points) and the duration of the breach. When the arriving data points fall below the threshold, exceed the threshold, or go outside the defined range for long enough, the threshold is said to be breached and the monitor transitions from *clear* into *alert* state. When the data points fall within the limits of the defined threshold, the monitor recovers and returns to clear state. Monitor states are used as factors in the evaluation of alarm states.

Monitoring System

A monitoring system is a set of software components that performs measurements and collects, stores, and interprets the monitored data. The system is optimized for efficient storage and prompt retrieval of monitoring metrics for visual inspection of timeseries as well as data point analysis for the purposes of alerting.

Many vendors have taken up the challenge of designing and implementing monitoring systems. A great deal of open source products are available for use and increasingly more cloud vendors offer monitoring and alerting as a service. Listing them here makes little sense as the list is very dynamic. Instead, I'll refer you to the Wikipedia article on comparing network monitoring systems (*http://bit.ly/RUbrWW*), which does a superb job comparing about 60 monitoring systems against one another and classifying each in around 17 categories based on supported features, mode of operation, and licensing.

It's good to ask the following questions when selecting a monitoring product:

- What are the fees and restrictions imposed by product's license?
- Was the solution designed with reliability and resilience in mind? If not, how much effort will go into monitoring the monitoring platform itself?
- Is it capable of juxtaposing timeseries from arbitrary metrics on the same plot as needed?
- Does it produce timeseries plots of fine enough granularity?

- Does its alerting platform empower experienced users to create sophisticated alarms?
- Does it offer an API access that lets you export gathered data for offline analysis?
- How difficult is it to scale it up as your system expands?
- How easily will you be able to migrate from it to another monitoring or alerting solution?

The vast majority of monitoring systems, including those listed in the article, share a similar high-level architecture and operate on very similar principles. Figure 1-1 illustrates the interactions between its components. The process starts with collection of input data. The agents gather and submit inputs to the monitoring system through its specialized write-only interface. The system stores data inputs in metrics and may submit fresh data points for evaluation of threshold breach conditions. When a threshold breach is detected, an alert may be sent to notify the operator about the fault. The operator analyzes timeseries plots and draws conclusions that lead to a mitigative action. Generally speaking, the process is broken down into three functional parts:

1. Data Collection

   The data about system's operations is collected by agents from servers, databases, and network equipment. The source of data are logs, device statistics, and system measurements. Collection agents group inputs into metrics and give them a set of properties that serve as an address in space and time. The inputs are later submitted to the monitoring system through an agreed-upon protocol and stored in the metrics database.

2. Data Aggregation and Storage

   Incoming data inputs are grouped and collated by their properties and subsequently stored in their respective metrics. Data inputs are retrieved from metrics and summarized by a summary statistic to yield a timeseries. Resulting timeseries data points are submitted one by one to an alarm evaluation engine and are checked for occurrences of anomalous conditions. When such conditions are detected, an alarm goes off and dispatches an alert to the operator.

3. Presentation

   The operator may generate timeseries plots of selected timeseries as a way of gaining an overview of the current state or in response to receiving an alert. When a fault is identified and an appropriate mitigative action is carried out, the graphs should give immediate feedback and reflect the degree to which the corrective action has helped. When no improvement is observed, further intervention may be necessary.

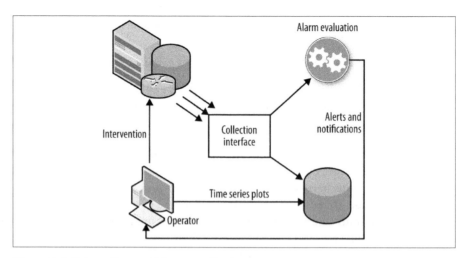

Figure 1-1. Interactions within a monitoring system

A monitoring system provides a point of reference for all operators. Its benefits are most pronounced in mature organizations where infrastructure teams, systems engineering, application developers and ops are enabled to interact freely, exchange observations and reassign responsibilities. Having a single point of reference for all teams significantly boosts the efficacy of detection and mitigation. Chapter 2 discusses monitoring in depth.

The Process of Alerting

Human operators play a central role in system monitoring. The process starts with establishing the system's baseline, that is, gathering information about the levels of performance and system behavior under normal conditions. This information serves as a starting point for the creation of an initial alerting configuration. The initial setup attempts to define abnormal conditions by defining thresholds for exceptional metric values.

Ideally, alarms should generate alerts only in response to actual defects that burden normal system operation. Unfortunately, that's not always the case.

When the thresholds are set up too liberally, legitimate problems may not be detected in time and the system runs a greater risk of performance degradation, which in the end may lead to system downtime. When the problems are eventually discovered and mitigated, the alerting configuration ought to be tightened to prevent the recurrence of costly outages.

Alarm monitors can also be created with unnecessarily sensitive thresholds, leading to a high likelihood that an alarm will be triggered by normal system operation. In such scenarios, the alarms will generate alerts when no harm is done. Once again, the baseline should then be reevaluated and respective monitors adjusted to improve detectability of real issues.

Most alarms, however, do go off for a valid reason and identify faults that can be mitigated. When that happens, an operator investigates the problem, starting with the metric that triggered the threshold breach condition and reasoning backwards in his search for a cause. When a satisfactory explanation is found and mitigative measures are taken to put the system back in equilibrium, the metrics reflect that and the alarm transitions back into the clear state. If the metrics do not reveal any improvement, that raises questions about the effectiveness of the mitigation and an alternative action might need to be taken to combat the problem fully.

Once more, after a successful recovery, the behavior of system metrics might improve enough to warrant yet another baseline recalculation and subsequent adjustment of the alarm configuration (Figure 1-2).

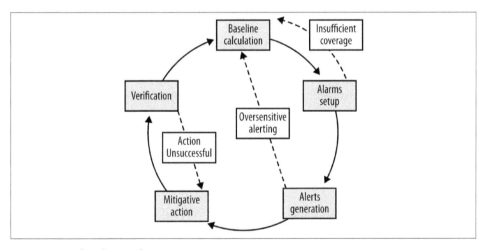

Figure 1-2. The alerting loop

Issue Tracking

An Issue Tracking System (ITS) is a database of reported problems recorded in the form of tickets. It facilitates prioritization and adequate tracking of reported problems as well as enabling the efficient collaboration between an arbitrary number of individuals and teams. Alerts often take the form of tickets, and therefore their role in prioritization and event response is very relevant to the process of alerting.

Tickets and queues

A ticket is a description of a problem with a chronological record of actions taken in attempt to resolve it.

Tickets are an extremely convenient mechanism for prioritizing incoming issues and enabling collaboration between multiple team members. They may be filed by humans or generated by automated processes, such as alarms attached to metric monitors. Either way, they are indispensable in helping to resolve problems and serve as a central point of reference for all parties involved in the resolution process. New information is appended to the ticket through updates. The most recent update reflects the latest state of the ticket. When a solution to the problem is found and applied, the ticket is archived and its state changes from "open" to "resolved."

Every ticket comes with a title outlining symptoms of the reported problem, some more detailed description, and an assigned severity. Typically, the severity level falls into one of four or five possible categories: urgent, high, normal, low, and, optionally, trivial. Chapter 3 describes the process of selecting the right priority. Tickets also have a set of miscellaneous properties, such as information about the person making the request, as well as a set of timestamps recording creation and modification dates, which are all used in the process of reporting.

The operator dealing with tickets is expected to work on them in order of priority from most to least severe. To assist the operator, the tickets are placed in priority queues. Each ticket queue is a database query that returns a list of ticket entries sorted by a set of predefined criteria. Most commonly, the list is sorted by priority in descending order and, among priorities, by date from oldest to newest.

Depending on the structure and size of the organization, an ITS may host from one to many hundreds of ticket queues. Tickets are reassigned between queues to signal transfer of responsibility for issue resolution. A team may own a number of queues, each for a separate breed of tickets.

Tickets resolved over time are a spontaneously created body of knowledge, with valuable information about the system problems, the sources of the problems, solutions for mitigation, and the quality of work carried out by the operators in resolving the problems. Practical ticket mining techniques are described in Chapter 7.

The Challenges

It is commonly believed that for monitoring to be effective it has to take conscious, continuously applied effort. Monitoring is not a trivial process and there are many facets to it. Sometimes the priorities must be balanced. It is true that an ad hoc approach will often require more effort than necessary, but with good preparation monitoring can become effortless. Let's look at some factors that make monitoring difficult.

Baselining

The problem with baselines is not that they are hard to establish, but that they are volatile. There are few areas for which the sentence *"nothing endures but change"* is more valid than for information systems. Hardware gets faster, software has fewer bugs, the infrastructure becomes more reliable. Sometimes software architects trade off the use of one resource for another, other times they give up a feature to focus on the core functionality. The implication of all that on monitoring and alerting is that alarms very quickly become stale and meaningless, and their maintenance adds to the operational burden.

Coverage

Full monitoring coverage should follow a system's expansion and structural changes, but that's not always the case. More commonly, the configurations are set up at the start and revisited only when it is absolutely necessary, or—worse yet—when the configurations are so out of date that real problems start getting noticed by end users. Maintaining full monitoring coverage, which is essential to detecting problems, is often neglected until it's too late.

Manageability

Large monitoring configurations include tens of thousands of metrics and thousands of alarms. Complex setups are not only expensive to maintain in terms of manual labor, but are also prone to human misinterpretation and oversight. Without a proper systematic approach and rich instrumentation, the configurations will keep becoming increasingly inconsistent and extremely hard to manage.

Accuracy

Sometimes faults will remain undetected, whereas other times alarms will go off despite no immediate or eventual danger of noticeable impact. Reducing the incidence of both kinds of errors is a constant battle, often requiring decisions that might seem counterintuitive at the beginning. But this battle is far from being lost!

Context

Monitoring's main objective is to identify and pinpoint the source of problems in a timely manner. Time is too precious and there is not enough of it for in-depth analysis. In order for complex data to be presented efficiently, large sets of numbers must be reduced to single numeric values or classified into a finite number of buckets. As a consequence, the person observing plots must make accurate assumptions based on a thorough understanding of the underlying data, their method of collection, and their source. Where do the inputs come from? In what proportions? What is the distribution of the values? Where are the limits? Correct interpretation requires in-depth knowledge of the system, which monitoring itself does not provide.

Human Nature

In striving for results, humans often see what they want rather than what's actually there. All too often, important pieces of information get discarded as outliers or as having negligible impact. Operators get away with neglecting outliers most of the time, but on rare occasions, especially at a large scale, neglecting these information-rich outliers may result in a high visibility outage. In addition, humans are terrible intuitive statisticians. We are prone to setting round thresholds, with a particular fondness for powers of 10, and we easily lose the sense of proportion.

Important Terms

There is a fair amount of discrepancy in the use of monitoring vocabulary. Many organizations, especially those with long established culture, use specific monitoring terms interchangeably. I'd like to close this chapter with a short glossary of the most important terms used throughout the book. I hope it will help to avoid some of the confusion.

Agent

A software process that continuously records data inputs and reports them to a monitoring system.

Alarm

A piece of configuration describing an undesirable condition and alerts issued in response to it.

Alert

A notification message informing about a change of state, typically signifying a potential problem.

Alerting

The process of configuring alarms and alerts.

Data Input

A numeric value with an accompanying set of properties gathered at the source of the measurement by a monitoring agent.

Data Point

A numeric value summarizing one or multiple data inputs reported in a defined time interval. A series of data points makes up a timeseries.

Metric

A collection of data inputs described by a set of properties. Timeseries are often mistakenly referred to as metrics. Monitoring metrics should not be confused with *performance metrics* either, which are a set of high level business performance indicators.

Monitor

A process evaluating the most recent data points on a timeseries for threshold fit. This is an integral part of an alarm.

Monitoring

The process of collecting and retrieving relevant data describing a change of state.

Timeseries

A list of data points sorted in natural temporal order, most commonly presented on a plot.

## CHAPTER 2

Monitoring

Some benefits of monitoring are immediate, such as early detection, evidence-based decision making, and automation. But its full value extends beyond that. Monitoring plays a central role in the absorption of job knowledge and driving innovation. You can't manage what you don't measure. A widely deployed monitoring solution keeps everyone on the same page. Timeseries plots allow for the exchange of complex ideas that would otherwise take a thousand words. Monitoring adds great value to the system and helps to foster the culture of rapid and informed learning.

The Building Blocks

The main purpose of monitoring is to gain near real-time insight into the current state of the system, in the context of its recent performance. The extracted information helps to answer many important questions, assists in the verification of nonstandard behavior, lets you drill down for more information on an issue that has been reported, and helps you estimate the capacity of the system. Before I move on to discussing all these useful aspects, I think it will help if I discuss the fundamental building blocks of a system from the bottom up.

Data Collection

The process of monitoring starts with gathering data by collection agents, specialized software programs running on monitored entities such as hosts, databases, or network devices. Agents capture meaningful system information, encapsulate it into quantitative data inputs, and then report these data inputs to the monitoring system at regular intervals. The inputs are then collated and aggregated into metrics to be presented as data points on a timeseries at a later stage. Input collection may be a continuous process or it may occur periodically at even time intervals, depending on the nature of the measurement and the cost of the resources involved in data collection.

Data collection agents can be categorized into the following groups:

White-box
Log parsers

These extract specific information from log entries, such as the status codes and response times of requests from a web server log.

Log scanners

These count occurrences of strings in log files, defined by regular expressions. For instance, to look for both regular errors and critical errors, you can check the number of occurrences of the regex "ERROR|CRITICAL" in a log file.

Interface readers

These read and interpret system and device interfaces. Examples include readings of CPU utilization from a Linux */proc* pseudo-filesystem and readings of temperature or humidity from specialized devices.

Black-box
Probers

These run outside the monitored system and send requests to the system to check its response, such as ping requests or HTTP calls to a website to verify availability.

Sniffers

These monitor network interfaces and analyze traffic statistics such as number of transmitted packets, broken down by protocol.

Monitoring Overhead and the Observer Effect

Agents are processes, and as such they consume a small portion of the resources of the monitored entity. This is known as monitoring overhead, a small price to pay for data collection work. This overhead is not to be confused with the Observer Effect, which refers to a change in behavior of the observed entity when that one is being monitored.

Agents might generate the Observer Effect if they alter the state of the monitored object or when data collection intensifies or weakens based on the result of measurement. For instance, suppose that an agent measures performance of some object every 60 seconds under normal operation, but when measurements exceed expected bounds the agent's logic instructs it to start probing once every second, in the hope of reporting more granular results. This approach largely intensifies the frequency of probing, for which proportionally more resources are consumed. The introduced Observer Effect likely exacerbates the problem.

It is important to remember that monitoring agents ought to keep their logic simple and do two things really well: gather data inputs and push them to the monitoring system. Any additional features introduce unnecessary variation into the process of investigation and detection.

Before the data collection can take place, agents must be deployed to the monitored entities system-wide. However, in some circumstances, it might be desirable to monitor remote entities without the use of deployable agents. This alternative approach is referred to as *agentless data collection*, during which the data is transmitted from the monitored entity through an agreed protocol and is interpreted outside the monitored system.

You might want to resort to agentless monitoring in systems with heavy restrictions on custom software deployments, such as proprietary systems that disallow custom additions, legacy systems that don't support the execution of agents, and high-security systems with restrictions imposed by policy.

Examples of agentless data collection include:

- Gathering statistics from proprietary operating systems running on networking gear via Simple Network Management Protocol (SNMP).
- Periodically executing diagnostic commands via SSH and parsing the output.
- Mounting the */proc* on Linux remotely via sshfs for local interpretation.

Agentless monitoring comes with a couple of disadvantages:

- Network link outages between the monitored and the interpreting entity can result in missing data points.
- There is additional overhead, as the data must first get transferred to the interpreting entity, where the inputs are extracted.

Coverage

Complete monitoring should cover three major groups of metrics: resource availability, software performance, and, where applicable, user behavior. The metrics for all groups should be retrievable as a timeseries through a common interface that allows for effective identification of problem sources by correlating the timeseries of neighboring layers in a system stack. Full monitoring coverage spans networking, hardware, OS, middleware, the application, and a set of key performance indicators. Figure 2-1 illustrates the layers of coverage in a system stack.

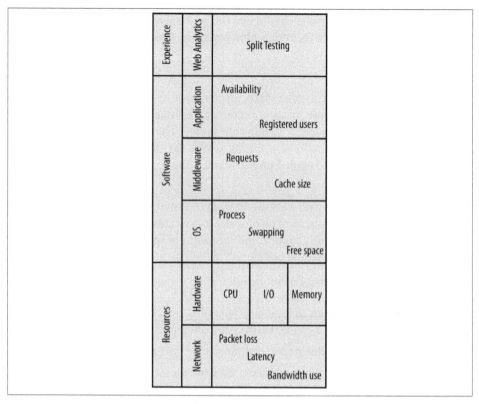

Figure 2-1. Monitoring coverage of system stack

Resources

Every action in the system costs CPU cycles. Most require memory, information exchange takes up bandwidth, data takes storage space, and communication between devices consumes I/O throughput. Resource usage patterns change with load. Large systems with human users tend to follow load patterns based on circadian rhythm with increased consumption of resources during the day and minimal utilization at night. It is important to realize what typical usage patterns are. Monitoring resource utilization helps you do that. Networking and computational resources require close and constant attention.

Data on resource utilization and availability can be collected directly from devices providing the resources. Usage levels are reported in the form of statistics from drivers through a programmable interface.

Network. Data delivered over the network travels with a sometimes noticeable latency: the time delay caused by digital processing and physical transport media. A network link also has a limited throughput, defined as the amount of information conveyed per unit of time. Latency must be kept to a minimum and the higher the throughput the better. Transmission disruptions can be expressed in terms of increased latency and reduced throughput.

Because computer networks are central to the idea of distributed computing, any network disruptions will inevitably be manifested in the overall system's performance. Applications are designed with an assumption that the network simply works, but in reality it's dangerous to take this for granted. System performance problems resulting from network dysfunction have been succinctly captured in the set of *Fallacies of Distributed Computing* formulated in the nineties by L. Peter Deutsch. In essence, packet loss will take place, network latency will affect the application's performance, and network bandwidth will become limited. For these reasons, the network must be monitored closely.

Computational resources. The basic currency in the world of information systems is a unit of capacity. The cost of any user activity can be expressed in terms of the resources it uses. But overdrafts of this currency are not allowed, which is why it is so important to keep a close eye on resource saturation at all times.

A typical computational action in a web service environment is a request. Every request takes resources: at a minimum it consumes memory and CPU cycles, but frequently it also reads and writes some data to other devices such as disk drives, introducing further I/O cost.

The depletion of any resource required to serve a request leads to creation of the so-called performance bottleneck. Usage patterns cannot be predicted with 100% reliability and resource shortages may not always be prevented by accurate capacity planning or dynamic allocation of instances in the cloud. Remember that meeting the load with additional capacity is not always desirable. Consider *Denial of Service* (DoS) attacks, where the attacker's objective is to shut down the service by driving the saturation of the scarcest resource it can manipulate. Monitoring computational resources in the context of system use is necessary to discern patterns and react accordingly.

Solution stack

A solution stack commonly consists of three parts: the operating system (OS), middleware, and an application running on top. Each layer generates information about the state of each component. It is important to have an overview of and collect metrics for all components of the solution stack, because faults can arise at any layer. The more software metrics that are reported, the more conclusions you can draw without digging into logs. There is nothing wrong with log analysis—logs will contain crucial, precise information that may never make it into a timeseries—but plotting metrics is much faster, and most of the time you don't need the precise data logs yield, while you almost always need to see the big picture fast.

Operating system. While tightly bound to resource utilization, operating system monitoring examines resource usage more at the software level: it aims to find out how efficiently resources are being used, in what proportions, and by whom. Typically, OS level metrics report on the proportion of user-to-system CPU time; virtual memory management including swapping and memory statistics; process management, including context switching and waiting queue states; and finally filesystem level statistics like inode information.

Various operating systems respond differently to different usage patterns, and within any OS many parameters are tunable. Fine tuning the OS according to your use case may result in better performance, which will obviously be reflected in monitoring metrics.

Early indications of physical hardware failures sometimes get reported in OS level logs, which may enable operators to act preventively before a machine fails in production.

Middleware. On top of the OS, the middleware layer serves as the platform for an application. It provides a standard set of combinable, purpose-specific software components which, put together, act as the engine of the solution. Middleware in distributed computing includes software web servers and application server frameworks. For monitoring purposes, these gather per-request information, keeping track of the amount of open sessions and states of transactions.

Application. Application metrics contain information specific to the operation and state of the application only. They often introduce high-level abstract constructs specific to the domain of the application. Thus, a batch processing system can express a batch in terms of size and number of items contained. A content management system can describe a modification operation by the extent of changes (major or minor), type (addition, deletion, or both), the time a person took to update content, etc.

Application inputs may vary from relatively few long-lived events (e.g., open sessions) to an extremely large number of short-lived metrics (such as ad impressions). In both cases it is usually appropriate to measure their turnaround times and express them as delay measurements. The application-level load measurements can be expressed through input levels (i.e., incoming traffic and number of submitted inputs).

Availability is also measured at the application level of the stack. A failure in any of the underlying layers of the system stack takes away from the overall availability of your system. Therefore, for an availability metric to be meaningful, it must be recorded from external locations so the network is measured as well.

User experience

Finally, monitoring user behavior is carried out with web analytics software in order to answer questions about user experience. Classic user behavior metrics used in websites are the average time spent on the site and the percentage of returning visitors. User behavior monitoring is a broad subject and is beyond the scope of this book.

Metrics

Monitoring metrics are collections of numeric data inputs organized in groups of consecutive, chronologically ordered lists. Each data input consists of a recorded measurement value, the timestamp at which the measurement took place, and a set of properties describing it.

When data inputs from a metric are segmented into fixed time intervals and summarized by a mathematical transformation in some meaningful way, they can be presented as a timeseries and interpreted on two-dimensional plots.

The length of data point intervals, also referred to as *time granularity*, depends on types of measurements and the kind of information that is to be extracted. Common intervals include 1, 5, 15, and 60 minutes, but it is also possible to render intervals as granular as one second and as coarse one day.

The single most important advantage of using timeseries for monitoring is their property of accurately illustrating the process of change in a context of historical data. They are an indispensable tool for finding the answer to the critical question: what has changed and when?

Timeseries are two-dimensional with data on the y-axis and time on the x-axis. This means that any two independent timeseries will always share one dimension—time. This way, plotting data from multiple metrics against one another adds just a single layer of complexity at a time to the chart. For that reason, timeseries provide an efficient means of highlighting correlative relationships between data from many sources, such as interlayer dependencies in a software stack.

Summary statistics

Monitoring metrics store data inputs and describe their properties. Generating and plotting a timeseries involves retrieving a subset of data inputs by specifying a set of properties (for example, hostname, group), dividing them into evenly spaced time intervals, and mathematically summarizing data inputs in each interval. This is done with the use of summary statistics. Commonly used summary statistics are:

n

The count of inputs per interval

sum

Sum of values from all inputs

avg

Mean value for all inputs (*sum / n*)

p0-p100

Percentiles (0-100) of the input values including min (*p0*) and max (*p100*) values as well as the median (*p50*)

deviation

Standard deviation from the average in the distribution of the collected inputs

Summary statistics describe observed input sets by their centers (average or median), the total (*sum, n*), and the distribution and spread (percentiles and deviations). They can summarize huge data sets in a compact and concise way. Turning many numbers into a single one does cause information loss, but the summary is usually accurate enough to draw reliable conclusions. Figure 2-2 shows how data from an irregular data set are represented through summary statistics.

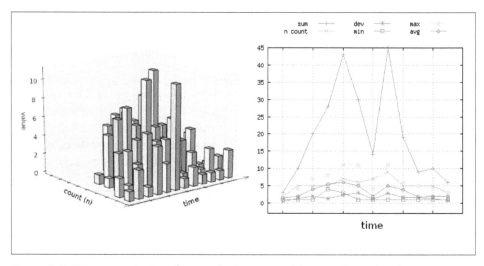

Figure 2-2. 3D representation of a sample data set and its two dimensional summary

Frequency distribution and percentiles. Frequency distribution is a summary of a data set that combines numeric items (a process called *binning*) into groups and presents the groups in manner that lets you quickly see their relative size. The distribution is most commonly illustrated in a histogram, as depicted on Figure 2-3. The x-axis here is *not* a timeline, as it is when presenting a timeseries. The left side of Figure 2-3, labeled "milliseconds," answers the question "How many transactions took 300 milliseconds, compared to 100 milliseconds, etc.?"

Histograms often fall along a normal distribution, with their bins fitting right under the famous Gaussian curve. But system data is usually not that regular and typically displays a long right tail; that is, the distribution is skewed to the left. There is a simple reason for that: the lower limit on performance is a hard one—it can't break the laws of physics. Think of latency, for instance: the best case scenario turnaround time must always be more than zero time units. Its upper limit, on the other hand, is a soft one—theoretically, you could wait forever.

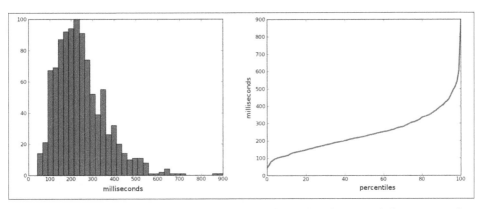

Figure 2-3. Histogram and percentile plot describing distribution of data inputs that make up data points on timeseries

Summary statistics plotted as data points over time are convenient for observing change, but timeseries don't necessarily reveal the true nature of the data.

You can extract raw data inputs from offline log analysis and present them on a histogram to show their relative frequency. This information gives operators a good idea of what value to expect from a typical input and what the input distribution looks like behind each summarized data point.

An alternative way to summarize frequency distribution is a percentile plot. For any set of inputs, a percentile is a real number in the range of 0 to 100 with a corresponding value from that set. The number at a particular percentile shows how many values are smaller than the value of that percentile.

Percentiles get calculated by sorting the set of inputs by value in ascending order, finding the rank for a given percentile (that is, the address of the value in the sorted list), and looking up the value by rank.

The 0th percentile is the measurement of the lowest value (the first element in a sorted list, *min*), and the 100th percentile is the maximum recorded value (the last element in the list, *max*). The 50th percentile or *p50* is commonly referred to as the *median*, and stands for the middle value in the set. Percentiles make distribution easy to interpret; for example, for measuring response time a *p98* value of 3 seconds means that 98% of all requests completed in 3 seconds or less. Conversely, 2% of the slowest requests took 3 seconds or more.

Rate of change. Rate of change illustrates the degree of change between data points on a timeseries or other curve. Effectively, where the slope of the original timeseries plot is rising, its rate of change has positive values. Conversely, when the slope descends, the values on the rate of change series are negative. The rate of change derived from a timeseries can be presented as another timeseries.

Rate of change is a useful conceptual tool for illustrating levels of growth or decline over time. It is used extensively with counter metrics (discussed further) to express number of counter increments per time interval.

Time granularity

Data points in a timeseries are presented at a fixed time granularity. Fine granularity translates to short data point periods. The coarser the granularity, the longer the period.

Fine granularity metrics tend to reveal the exact time of an event and are therefore useful for finding direction in causal relationships, as well as describing timelines. They might, however, be more expensive to store. Coarse granularity metrics, on the other hand, are much more suited for illustrating trends.

Selecting the right granularity to present a metric is important for accurate interpretation of data. Both too granular and very coarse measurements may obscure the point you're trying to convey.

Some monitoring systems lock the user into using predefined constant intervals, whereas others allow the user to specify arbitrary periods. However, some minimum interval is always required. Even if we were able to present events on a continuous time scale (with an infinitesimally fine granularity), it would probably not be very helpful. In the real world, no two events happen at the exact same time, so recording that on a continuous scale would never make the event count stack up on the plot. In other words, the maximum event count on our continuous timeseries would never exceed 1 at any given data point. Going to the other extreme, if the data point interval is extremely long, such as one year, the output will be a huge collection of event occurrences. That can be somewhat useful for purposes of data analysis but not for monitoring.

Metric aggregation

In distributed systems, data inputs for the same metric come from many sources. Think of a group of web servers behind a load balancer, reporting statistics about requests being served. One way to view the request data is in the form of multiple timeseries, one for each web server, plotted out against each other. However, aggregation could combine the results from the web servers into a single timeseries with a total of all requests.

Aggregation enables you to get an overview of the data and simplifies the chart, but the ability to drill down to view each source of data is no less important. Suppose one of the servers stops taking requests. It will either report zero-valued data points or stop sending inputs altogether. The fault can be detected by looking at the individual server metrics, but it wouldn't necessarily show on the aggregated plot.

Many faults, however, are a lot subtler than that and manifest themselves through slight depressions in the number of requests rather than their complete disappearance. In these cases, it is also desirable to aggregate data points from all sources and present them as a single metric to show the cumulative effect.

Metric aggregation is not to be confused with alarm aggregation, discussed in more detail in Chapter 3.

Example: Inputs, Metrics, and Timeseries

I created some sample data by sending ICMP echo requests every second for a period of one hour and recording the round-trip time for each request. Figure 2-4 shows a 3D plot of latency. The plot includes all data inputs in their unreduced form. Two clusters of very high latency are visible: one peaking at 177ms between 10 and 20 seconds of minute 14, and the other peaking at 122ms between 40 and 50 seconds of minute 40. Their empty bars signify packet loss.

The plot on Figure 2-5 was created from the same set of inputs as that on Figure 2-4. The inputs were gathered in active mode and served as a basis for two separate multi-N metrics, one for packet loss and one for latency. Both are presented as timeseries with data points at one-minute intervals and summarized by arithmetic mean.

This time we see latency as a line with crosses (green). Each cross marks one data point, summarized from measurements taken at the interval of one minute. The y-axis of this line is measured by the numbers on the left-hand side of the figure. Packet loss is shown as a plain red line). The y-axis for packet loss is measured by the numbers on the right-hand side of the figure, which range from 0 (no packet loss, which is the case most of the time) to 0.035 (3.5% packet loss).

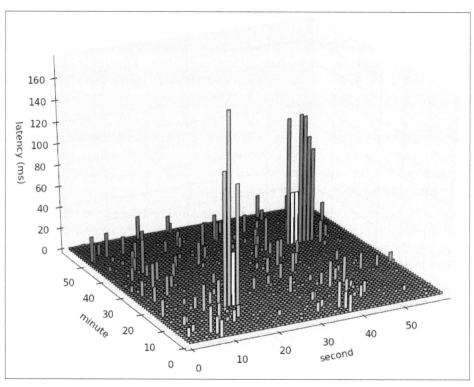

Figure 2-4. ICMP echo messages sent every second for a duration of one hour

Because the data is chunked by minute, and the test sent a packet once per second, the packet loss metric is calculated by dividing the number of packets lost during a minute by 60. The two spikes in packet loss are at minute 14, where it reached 0.017 (1.7%), denoting that 1 out of 60 inputs was lost, and almost 3.5% at minute 40, which denotes 2 lost packets.

Overall, Figure 2-5 illustrates how you can trade off the loss of some detail in order to get a quicker grasp of underlying issues.

Understanding Metrics

A solid understanding of data presented in metrics is essential to drawing reliable conclusions from timeseries plots. Knowing which category a metric belongs to and where its data originates is helpful in realizing the impact of pattern shifts and presenting the information in the most conclusive ways. Some summary statistics emphasize the key insight better than others, and the same data may appear dissimilar when displayed at a different time granularity. Realizing differences of that sort assists in constructing plots that clearly convey the point.

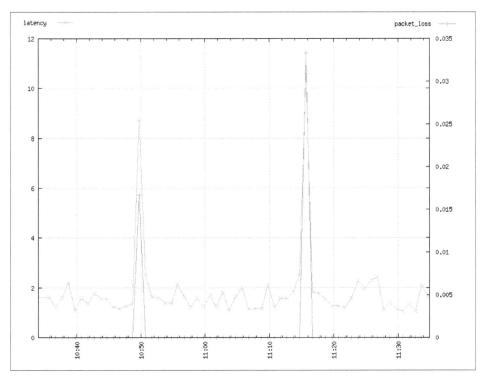

Figure 2-5. The plot of average latency and packet loss

This section breaks down the interpretation of metrics by looking at their basic properties. Looking at metrics in this way should enable you to make reliable assumptions about the data and their origin and understand likely changes in metric behavior. But hey, don't just take my word for it. Visit RRDTool Gallery (*http://oss.oetiker.ch/rrdtool/gallery/*). The page contains tens of performance graphs and timeseries examples submitted by RDDTool users from around the globe. Try going there before and after reading this section. Are you able to extract some more meaning the second time?

Type of unit

Each metric can be seen in three general ways based on the type of its units.

Amount

A collection of discrete or continuous values resulting from inputs; examples include number of matches in a search result, packet size, price, free disk space.

This group of metrics is by far the most common. Resulting data plotted as timeseries illustrates operational flow and states. Amounts are typically recorded at all levels of the software stack.

Units: bytes, kilograms, price, sum of returned items.

Time Delay
> An amount of time required for an action to complete; examples include latency, web request response time, ICMP round-trip time, time spent by a user on the website.
>
> Just like amounts, delays are typically recorded at all levels and play a crucial role in performance monitoring due to the immediate effect of response times on user experience. Resulting data points are almost always a blend of multiple inputs that happened in a given time period. Typically, their average, median, and high percentile values are watched most closely.
>
> Units: milliseconds, seconds, minutes, hours, days, CPU cycles.

Amount per Time
> Discrete or continuous amounts flowing through the system per unit of time, more generally referred to as throughput; examples include bit rate and Input/Output Operations Per Second (IOPS).
>
> Such metrics are suitable for monitoring small data bits produced in big amounts with high potential variability of values. They are most commonly used for monitoring lower level metrics such as hardware device statistics. Typically, the underlying hardware device has a built-in mechanism for keeping track of and reporting on the flow of throughput. In such cases, amount per time metrics represent one input per data point: that is, the device was queried for its state once in a given data point period. In other cases, where multiple inputs are available per data point, the variability of throughput can be observed through input distribution via use of percentiles, just as in case of the previous two types.
>
> Units: bits per second, IOPS, miles per hour.

Let me illustrate this classification with an example of requests to a web server.

A web server accepts HTTP requests and issues a response to each of them that takes a non-zero amount of time. The duration dependent on the size of the request.

Suppose the server accepts up to 15 simultaneous requests and that each request takes on average 200 ms to complete. Requests may come at different times and their duration may vary, but let's assume that the server can safely take 75 requests per second. All three types of metrics could find application here:

- Amount: Request size, or the record of each request's magnitude in bytes. The metric can be interpreted in terms of multiple summary statistics:
    - The sum of inputs reveals the total size of incoming user data. This information can later be used for billing purposes.

— The *avg*, *p0*, *p50*, and *p100* carry information about the variability of request sizes, revealing the average, smallest, most typical, and largest values respectively. This information about distribution of request sizes can be used for stress testing and capacity planning.

- Time Delay: Response time, or amount of time necessary for a request to complete. Interesting summary statistics include the average, the fluctuation of which reveals sudden changes in the underlying distribution, and *p99*, which holds the time of the slowest 1% of all responses.

- Amount per Time: Number of requests per second, the effective throughput of requests. Assuming that the inputs are measured every second to construct one-minute data points, *p100* reveals the maximum number of requests per second. When this number approaches the defined limit of approximately 75 requests per second, a degradation of user experience might be observed; in the absence of a queuing mechanism, the requests will have to be dropped and the user will be forced to retry them.

In this particular case, there exists a strong correlation between all three measurements. The first two are positively correlated: the larger the request, the longer the response time. The amount per time metric and the other two are negatively correlated: the bigger the requests and thus the longer the responses, the fewer requests per second may be accepted.

Data Collection Mode

Data collection agents can operate in two modes, active or passive, depending on the actions taken to extract the data.

Active

An active monitoring entity proactively issues test requests to gather state and health information; examples include an ICMP ping request or an HTTP GET health probe.

Active monitoring introduces overhead into the net cost of system operation. The overhead is not usually monitored itself, but the operator should be aware of the proportion of introduced cost to the overall cost of normal system operation. When possible, monitoring impact should be kept at negligible levels.

Passive

In passive monitoring, the agent watches the flow of data and gathers statistics without introducing any cost into the system. In monitoring networks, the data is gathered by reading statistics from network gear and through the use of packet sniffers. The resulting information yields the number of transmitted packets and proportion of traffic divided into OSI model.

Data Source

Another way to classify measurements is by the locus of the data gathering agent, internal or external.

Internal
> Measurements are gathered within the system (log data, device statistics).
>
> Data inputs are collected internally with the help of agents executed continuously or at specific intervals and reporting statistics read from system's interfaces such as the */proc* filesystem in Linux. Centralized monitoring systems may also gather data in an agentless fashion by opening SSH sessions from their central location to a set of monitored destination hosts in order to read the statistics and interpret them locally.

External
> Measurements are gathered and reported by an external entity. External monitors typically operate in an active mode to establish availability (see the earlier examples of active monitoring), but they can also passively monitor data flow (through network sniffers inspecting and classifying traffic, for instance).
>
> External black-box monitoring is aimed at verifying the system's health. Health check agents send probes through system entry points to measure end-to-end availability.
>
> When the scale of the organization is significant enough, a special kind of external monitoring is possible through watching social networks. A huge number of results for "is Google down or is it just me" in a Twitter search query, for instance, might be an indication of problems with accessing the website.

Number of Inputs per Data Point

Metric measurements can be further divided into multiple subcategories based on the number of inputs required to construct a data point and the nature of the measurement.

Multi-N
> Data points for multi-N metrics are summary statistics combined from multiple processed inputs. The inputs get aggregated and the resulting data point contains a full set of useful summary statistics describing cumulative effects (sum, n), typical values (average, median) and distribution of the data (percentiles).
>
> Examples include bytes transferred, number of HTTP requests, average time on site, and *p99* of the response time.

Single-N or 1-N

Data points for these metrics require only a single input in order to construct a meaningful data point. In most cases, the metric illustrates state change over time. Although the schema of the data point may include the full set of summary statistics, the one and only recorded value will be assigned to all of them and n will be equal to 1.

Examples include IOPS, CPU utilization, and message count.

Type of Quantity

Metrics can also be interpreted by the type of quantity they represent.

Flow

This kind of metric records events and their properties.

Flow records a variable number of inputs per interval (that is, it is multi-N). The data is gathered from multiple sources and is summarized after being aggregated. A high variability of input values allows the viewer to draw conclusions from the distribution of inputs. High values of extreme percentiles are an early indication of changes, some of which could be interpreted as worrying.

Examples include the sizes of packets sent, prices of sold items, and response times for each request.

Throughput

This measures the rate of processing over a period of time.

Throughput metrics record continuity and intensity of flow. They are expressed in units per time and illustrate levels of resource consumption. Because throughput limits can be reliably tested and clearly defined, this type of metric is used for alarming on resource saturation and identifying bottlenecks.

Examples include bit rate and IOPS.

Stock

This indicates an accumulated quantity at a specific point in time.

Stock metrics are single-N. They record a single data input per data point interval. They are expressed in simple units of quantity and represent a total of the agglomerated value. The levels of stock may be changed by processes that are recorded by flow metrics, and the intensity of these changes is expressed by throughput metrics.

Examples include memory usage, free disk space, queue length, temperature, and volume level.

Availability

This measures the degree to which the expected result is returned.

The source of input for availability metrics are probes—requests issued proactively that return success on the receipt of an expected response or failure otherwise. Probes may be internal or external. As a multi-N metric, with low variability of input values (1 on success and 0 on failure), the average of inputs yields availability in percentage terms (a number ranging from 0.0 to 1.0).

Examples include HTTP GET requests expecting a 200 response code, ICMP ping results, and packet loss.

Timeseries Patterns

Data points on a time series follow patterns that strongly depend not only on the number and variability of recorded inputs but also on the temporal granularity and the properties of the selected summary statistic. The finer the temporal granularity, the more spiky the timeseries will appear, while series with coarser granularity demonstrate less variability of data point values. Summarizing multiple inputs with extreme percentiles also leads to higher variability (more fluctuations) than when summarizing with average. Analyzing timeseries in terms of their patterns is crucial in understanding their normal behavior and plays a role in selecting the right alerting strategy.

Figure 2-6 shows eight common patterns. We'll take a look at what each pattern indicates.

Spiky
> This is often found in flow and throughput metrics and can be attributed to high variability or burstiness of inputs: their sudden change in values or quantity. Spiky patterns are often noticed on metrics relating to bandwidth usage and computational resources that are prone to rapid changes in utilization patterns.

Steady
> This appears when data point values have a low variability at a non-zero level. Their value range is probably restrained from one side, for instance, by the laws of physics (latency, speed of light in glass) or a hard limit at 100%. This pattern is seen when measuring availability and underutilized resources. When no distinguishable trends are present, accurate alarm threshold values can be calculated from average and standard deviation.

Counter
> This is a special case that occurs with a stock metric, where a discrete value keeps increasing until it gets flushed. These metrics are a reflection of a counter variable plotted over time. Counters include records of event occurrences since a certain date or indicate an age, where the counter variable increases at a constant time interval, thus measuring the temporal distance since a point in time. Counters do not decrease, but they might get reset to 0. They are used for evidencing and predicting the necessity for maintenance. The record of counter's rate of change can be interpreted as a flow of incrementing events (see Flow).

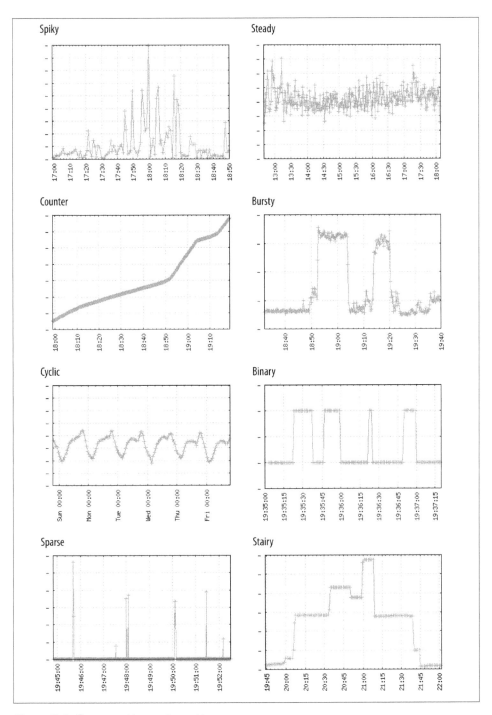

Figure 2-6. Common timeseries patterns

Examples include the number of seconds since last update (age in seconds) and the number of reboots since last filesystem check (usage-age).

Bursty

These metrics come as a result of an intermittent operation of system components, with extended periods of inactivity, as in the case of CPU utilization on batch processing systems such as map-reduce clusters. These jump up to almost 100% on the processing of a job, but stay low while awaiting submissions.

Cyclic

Series following sinusoidal patterns are subject to cycles. Virtually all metrics that come as a result of interactions with humans from a selected geolocation and at scale—for instance, website traffic—reflect humans' diurnal cycle with trends and seasonal effects.

Binary

These appear for availability metrics recording only two values: 1 and 0 on success and failure, or the presence and absence of events. Depending on the graphing system, a binary pattern can be presented as a square wave alternating between 0 and 1 or as a change of background color in affected temporal space (for instance, a red background for data points during which health probes failed).

Sparse

Sparse timeseries are ones whose metrics do not receive inputs at every interval. They record events that happen irregularly. Sparse timeseries can be subdivided into two categories: ones that record a value of zero even when no data inputs were reported, and ones that don't. In the former case, the recording of null values prevents interpolation between distant data points and makes the plots more interpretable, while the latter solution, less expensive to store and retrieve, may be a good fit for measurements taken on an irregular basis.

Sparse series are commonly used for recording errors and events unlikely to occur in normal operation.

Stairy

This pattern is observed when data points rise and fall sharply to stay at the same level for extended periods. It's commonly seen in stock metrics expressing level of consumption or activity, such as those that measure disk space, free memory, or number of processes running.

Drawing Conclusions from Timeseries Plots

Timeseries data are used to extract information about the past, present, and future. Real-time plots help to detect problems while they are occurring and help to confirm the validity of mitigative actions (for instance, in the case of high memory usage on a server and you watch it decrease after throttling an offending client IP). Data points gathered over time describe the operational system state in historical context, facilitating the detection of chronic problems that would otherwise not be classified as critical. In addition to preventative analysis, trends and seasonal variations are used for more accurate capacity planning.

Interpretation of Anomalies

Deviations of data points from standard patterns carry meaning that can be read like a symbolic language, its alphabet the spikes and dips, bursts and plummets, depressions and elevations, as well as flattening effects. The vocabulary of the language is somewhat limited and, therefore, the grammar must be based on strong contextual knowledge and a sense of proportion.

For a vast majority of timeseries, data point values change all the time, but only some of the time are they significant enough to be noticed and categorized as anomalies. Anomalous fluctuations can be considered in terms of their direction (rise or fall), magnitude of deviation (distance from the baseline), duration in data points, and progression.

Spikes and dips differ in direction (dips are negative spikes). They are short-lived (the timeseries recovers just after a few data points) and because of their short duration, they manifest no progression.

Elevation and depression also differ in direction, but take more data points to recover from and therefore may reveal different progression patterns: a sudden jump with sustained level, a linear increase/decline, or an exponential rise and fall.

The key to interpreting these sorts of fluctuations in a timeseries is to recognize the type of recorded quantity and the summary statistic used. Summary statistics can be binned in two groups: one describes the total of inputs as a bulk quantity, such as their sum or recorded amount (n), whereas the other describes how steady individual inputs are by means of average and percentile distribution.

The previous section described five quantity types: flow, stock, availability, and throughput.

Flow

Flow records some property shared by multiple events. The n statistic describes flow levels, that is, number of inflowing events per interval of time. Think again of requests incoming to a web server and their response times. The n statistic displays traffic levels. Sudden bursts and spikes can be attributed to client usage patterns. Given that not all requests have equal costs, the sum of request times can be interpreted as the total cost of operation expressed in computational hours. The average (*avg*) is the mean request time. An unsteady average hints at changes in the distribution of *input* values, typically a slowdown of a portion of requests.

Such a change is best highlighted by the use of high percentiles, such as *p95* or *p99*. Their exceptionally high values imply a shortage of resources or bandwidth saturation. If it's the former, spikes of *p99* should align with spikes of the sum (total computation time) and underlying CPU utilization stats. Although the average might be skewed by a fraction of slow requests, *p50* reliably describes typical user experience.

 The reason why it is more common to see distribution changes at higher rather than lower percentiles is that most metrics have hard limits for values at the lower end. At the same time, there is no restriction at the other end. Let me take network latency as an example: the lowest value is only as small as permitted by the laws of physics, while nothing prevents the response from taking arbitrarily long.

Stock

Stock quantities record information about capacity levels. They may pertain to storage, memory, or abstract constructs such as software queues. Stock metrics are inherently single-N, so their only valid summary statistic is the sum. Changes in data point values reflect inflows and outflows, which may be described in more detail by related flow metrics.

Suppose you monitor a data pipeline consisting of three components: a submitting entity, a queue, and a processing entity. The submitting entity enqueues requests and the processing entity dequeues and processes them sequentially. If the rate of submissions is lower than the rate of processing, the stock metric describing the queue level will remain at 0, occasionally reaching the value of 1. When the submission rate is higher than processing rate, the queue will increase steadily and a backlog will accumulate. If the submitting entity ceases its operation, the processing entity will drain the queue over time.

The counter type is a specialized case of a stock quantity, in which regular inflows are accepted, but the outflow is performed explicitly once in a while to flush the counter back to zero. As a stock metric, it is single-N and doesn't make any use of summary statistics. Deriving rate of change from a counter produces a timeseries for flow, describing the rate at which the counter increases.

In information systems, counters are often used to hold information about periodic maintenance, such as the number of partition mounts since the most recent filesystem check or the time in seconds since the most recent content update. Counters find their application also at the application level. Suppose you run an advertising platform, and display ads in rounds of 1000 impressions. When the counter reaches the impression limit, the counter is reset and the next ad is served.

The rate of increase should change with rates of Internet penetration. If the data points flatten out at a steady level for suspiciously long, the ads have probably been discontinued for some reason, and the issue might need to be investigated.

Consider another example. A fleet of machines requires regular maintenance that has to happen at least once every five days, but may happen more often. The way to keep track of time elapsed since the last maintenance is to record the difference between the current timestamp and the timestamp when the last maintenance completed. An alarm set up around such a metric's sum statistic with a threshold of 432000 seconds (five days) will issue a alert notification about a missed update.

Availability

Availability is a special case of a flow metric in which data inputs take one of two possible values, 0 and 1, corresponding to failure and success, respectively. When the total of collected inputs is averaged per data point, the data point takes a value of a fraction reflecting availability expressed in percentage terms. For example, if 9 out of 10 probes return success and 1 returns failure, the average availability for that data point equals:

$$(9*1 + 1*0) / 10 = 0.9 \text{ or } 90\%$$

Throughput

Throughput metrics record intensity of utilization and are expressed as average units of flow during a period of time or a percentage of total resource utilization per interval. Resource limitations are conveniently expressed in terms of their throughput, so this type of metric is perfectly suited for observing and alarming when resource saturation occurs. Examples of throughput metrics include CPU utilization, which really is a ratio of utilized clock ticks to all available ticks in a given interval of time, and the speed of transmission, or bit rate.

Applications of quantities

Table 2-1 summarizes the kinds of information extractable from combinations of summary statistics and quantity types.

Table 2-1. Information extractable from different types of metrics.

Type of Quantity	Measure of Total (n, sum)	Measure of Steadiness (average, percentiles)
Flow	Input levels, processing rate, total work or gain	Existence of bottlenecks, early indications of resource saturation, regularity of inputs

Type of Quantity	Measure of Total (n, sum)	Measure of Steadiness (average, percentiles)
Stock	Available space, freshness, state since last reset, continuity of operation	N/A
Availability	N/A	Level of availability, event incidence in percentage terms, content coverage
Throughput	N/A	Intensity of utilization, saturation, burstiness

Frequently Encountered Anomalies

We can now survey a few commonly seen patterns in the quantity data discussed in the previous section.

Flattening Effect

A *flattening effect* is manifested when the line on the plot reaches an artificially steady level, compared to historical data points (Figure 2-7). The effect may occur in many different types of metrics and for various reasons, but it almost never brings good news. It usually signifies a saturation of a resource or discontinuation of flow.

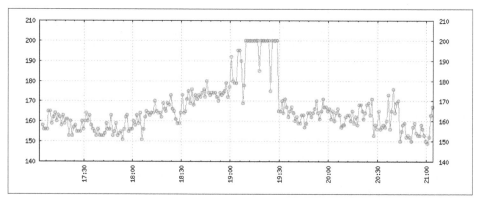

Figure 2-7. HTTP response time 99th percentile flattening at around 200 ms

Some concrete examples include:

- A sudden flattening on a counter metric indicates a discontinuation of flow. Its rate of change series is equal to flow metric continuously recording a 0 value.

- A flattening at 200 ms of *p99* in a response time metric may be a fallout of high packet loss combined with a retransmission timeout setting of 200 ms.

- Flat lines in CPU utilization point to resource saturation.

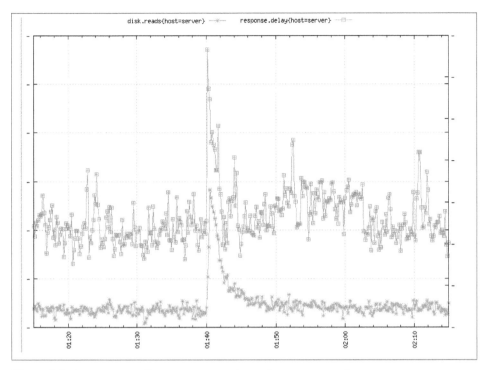

Figure 2-8. A warm-up effect on response time after content update

Warm-Up Effect

This effect occurs when a new server is put in service and the application has had no time yet to get up to speed. Due to initially empty system caches, the host processes data at a rate slower from the one observed in a steady running state. Warm-up effects manifest themselves as short-lived increases in response time (Figure 2-8).

Warming up a server before placing it in service is a tested method of avoiding degraded user experience. The idea is quite simple: simulate the load that the machine will handle and prepare the machine for operation by feeding the server with a sample of production traffic extracted from historical logs as it reenters the system.

Regular Anomalies

This consists of a returning record of anomalies, usually spikes, happening at equally spaced time intervals during resource-intensive automated processes (Figure 2-9).

The sources of the spike can be either internal or external. The fastest way to locate the internal cause is to check the crontab logs. Correlating the times of spikes with time-stamps in the logs uncovers the direct cause. Anomalies occurring at shorter intervals

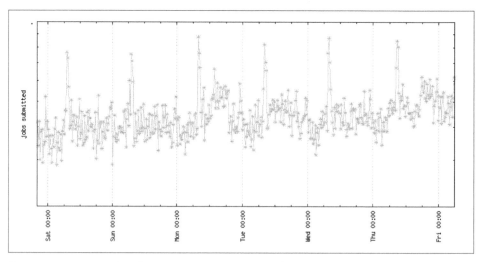

Figure 2-9. A cron job submitting computational tasks at 7:00 AM every day

up to an hour may be caused by a failing hardware device that is performing a periodic self-check or a retry. External causes are reflected in the input to the system, for example, intensified frequency or cost of incoming requests as observed during periodic web scraping.

Spikes During Troughs

On some occasions, traffic troughs correlate with high values of response time on extreme percentiles (deep in tail of input distribution) despite no performance degradation (Figure 2-10). During a trough, the system comes under very little load, so a trough should influence overall response times in a positive way—and it does. Still, mysterious indications of poor response time during a trough sometimes turn up, and feeble alerting configurations may set off alerts on this peculiarity. The effect might be a little counterintuitive at first, but it can be easily explained when one understands the nature of percentiles.

Consider a system that accepts 500 user queries per minute during its peak. Response times are monitored by watching the *p99* values on a minute-by-minute basis. Throughout the day, a healthcheck prober sends a single control request to the database every minute. It is very comprehensive and takes disproportionately longer than a normal user query. During a trough, the user query volume falls to the level of approximately 100 per one-minute data point, and this is when the data point values of the *p99* go high.

Let's take a look at what happens to *p99*: at peak, it represents the fastest out of five slowest queries (1% of 500). At trough, when the system gets only 100 queries a minute,

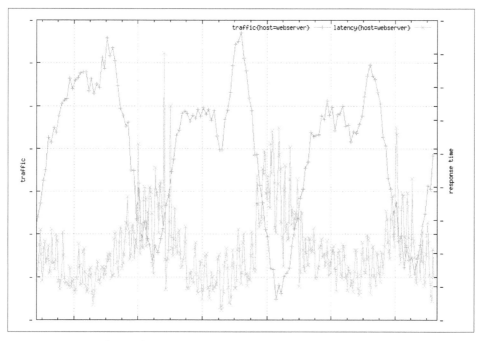

Figure 2-10. Correlation between trough and higher values at 95th percentile of response time

the slowest query makes it into *p99*. This is why *p99* jumps up so drastically. Only at trough does it include one exceptionally long running query. The general lesson one can derive from this example is to ensure that the underlying metric can supply your observation with a big enough sample size.

Determining Causality

To respond effectively to emergent system events, you must break through uncertainty in real time. The operator is expected to find the root of the problem by backward chaining from its symptoms to the cause and to subsequently apply mitigative action. When the process is broken down in three logical steps, the efficacy of investigation is significantly improved.

1. **Find correlation**. Most commonly, the process starts with the identification of undesired symptoms. To find the potential cause, gather and juxtapose timeseries from other system metrics that display similar levels of abnormality. Your timeseries

database might host thousands of metrics, but you need not look at all of them. It's important to remember that computer systems are organized in software stacks. Keep checking successively for metrics originating from layers or components surrounding the one that reveals symptoms.

Generic practical hints: for loss of availability, refer to network metrics. For problems with performance, check levels of resource utilization. For higher-level problems related specifically to a service, display metrics generated from system logs.

Found something? Great, but correlation does not imply causation, which brings up the next point.

2. **Establish direction.** Which is the horse and which is the cart? The need for a cause to precede its effects gives you the answer. Knowing that the problem comes either downstream or upstream (a layer above or below in the system stack), which anomalous timeseries recorded abnormal data points first? Here is where a timeseries of fine time granularity comes in very handy, as temporal precedence is usually a matter of seconds. If the time interval on your series is too coarse, you can still try to parse the logs. If that's not possible, maybe one of the outer-layer timeseries reveals less visible anomalies leading up to the trouble.

   At this point you should have identified one or more potential troublemakers among components of the system.

3. **Rule out confounding factors.** Okay, so you think you have it, but you can't be sure until your hypothesis is verified. Under exceptional circumstances, many components may display abnormal behavior, but it doesn't necessarily mean that they are contributing. If a number of potential sources of trouble are identified and the situation permits (if the fleet of hosts is big enough to allow for such experimentation), try to switch off or restart the suspected faulty components separately, each on its own host. This tests the hypothesis with all other things being equal. The machine that recovers after sample corrective action wins.

With time and experience, operators tend to develop strong intuition, which significantly expedites the identification of faults. To save time they have to make assumptions, and they will be right most of the time. On rare occasions, though, the assumptions prove wrong. At this point, backtracking and performing a full three-step search for cause might be a good idea.

How Causality Can Be Tricky to Find

I remember an interesting incident that happened during one of my on-call shifts. We were monitoring a fleet of front-end servers with web content generated on the back end. The back end continuously delivered the content in the form of updates to the front-end servers. The rate of updates was variable, but never reached alarming levels. The inexpensive process accepting updates on the front-end servers was commonly known to be absolutely independent from the web server part; that is, it could be shut down for extended periods of time without affecting the web server functionality in the slightest, almost as if it wasn't there at all. It was the web server that kept the machines busy, while the update processing component typically utilized CPU and I/O at negligible levels.

At one point we observed a huge increase in response latency at the web server. To establish the source of the symptoms we looked upstream and downstream, so we plotted traffic levels and CPU utilization along high latency on the graph. Our hope, as this chapter has stressed, was to conclusively determine the direction of the problem. High CPU utilization combined with low incoming traffic levels could imply that the problem is caused internally, while very high traffic levels would explain exceptionally high load reflected in CPU utilization. And in fact, the traffic graph showed five times the normal levels—easy! Some very aggressive client deserved to get blocked.

Remarkably, though, the CPU utilization graph started going up a moment before the client pounded the fleet with requests, as if anticipating and preparing for it (Figure 2-11). This suggested a downstream cause of the problem. Eventually, we correlated the initially high CPU levels with significantly more updates coming from the back end, which had some effect on the fleet's resource utilization. We dismissed this as a coincidence and blocked the offending client—the two systems are orthogonal, right?

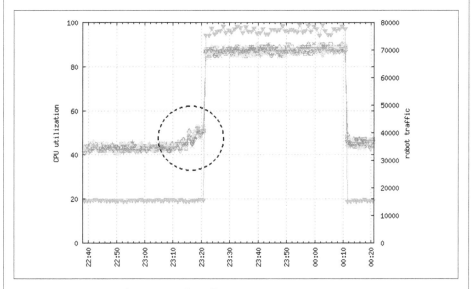

Figure 2-11. CPU utilization and traffic

The next day at a completely different time the same thing happened—five times the traffic, shortly after big amounts of updates had started to arrive. Okay, what were the odds of this double crisis?

The second time we didn't interpret the symptoms as coincidence. We switched off the component accepting updates and, to our surprise, the traffic went away. And turning it back on reinvited the traffic. How?

After some digging, it turned out that massive amounts of incoming back-end updates did have an impact on the system resources and contributed somewhat to raised response times. Most of the fleet continued to work at tolerable levels, but a few hosts responded really slowly. The web client in question was an automated process with an impatient retry mechanism, implemented to get the answers as quickly as possible. Essentially, when the client had not received a response fast enough, it assumed packet loss and issued another query. Then it used one of the two responses, whichever came first.

This had worked in the past, but now the system was genuinely slower because of the volume of incoming content updates. The client kept aggressively issuing requests up to five times, until it finally got an answer. This put additional load on the fleet already under strain, in effect causing increasingly more hosts to serve requests at really long response times. The harder the client pounded us with retries, the more hosts were going out of balance…

Of course, the problem had many facets: lack of a sufficient throttling mechanism, no admission control for incoming updates, and a bad retry mechanism on the part of the client, just to name a few factors. But that's not really unusual. Most outages do not have a single cause. What's interesting is the ease with which a plausible conclusion—in this case an external attack—got accepted immediately while the actual cause was discarded as a coincidence despite some evidence to the contrary.

Tracking causality is not the same as *root cause analysis* (RCA), but may serve as its starting point. Chapter 6 covers RCA in more detail.

Capturing the Daily Cycle, Trends, and Seasonal Changes

Most metrics record system state information pertaining to the current operation of the system. They are recorded "just in case" and are extremely useful for troubleshooting during outage responses. For instance, Figure 2-12 shows data points aggregated over one, twelve, and twenty-four hours.

As the system evolves, gets upgraded, and changes scale, the specific performance information becomes less and less relevant. This is why the retention period for resource utilization metrics rarely exceeds four weeks: a little bit of historical context is necessary to make reliable assumptions while troubleshooting, but retaining the I/O and CPU data for each individual host beyond this period is of little value.

However, metrics recording usage patterns encapsulate a more universal kind of information and should be retained much longer to be analyzed for trend and seasonality. The demand for the service your system provides is by and large dictated by its overall effectiveness and to a lesser extent by specific technical conditions. Your users will not

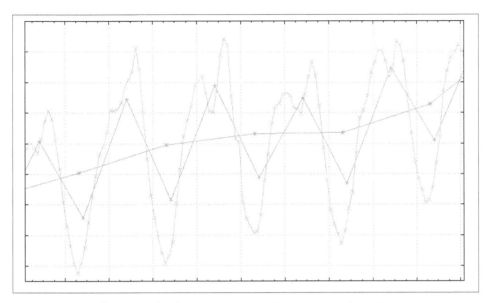

Figure 2-12. Traffic metric displaying a strong cyclic pattern and trend

care how effectively your resources are utilized as long as they are not affected by their shortage. When you measure demand progression, you should exclude inconsiderable variables that are present in resource utilization metrics. These variables include fleet size (because host utilization levels vary depending on the breadth of the fleet), hardware type, software efficacy, etc.

Systems with seasonal usage patterns must identify and capture demand indicators so you can plan capacity accurately. Planning is important because underutilizing resources is wasteful, but when there is not enough of them you're at risk of degraded performance and availability loss.

Non-realtime data pipelines and batch processing systems may defer excess load for less busy periods, so the problem is most pronounced for interactive systems, such as most websites.

First of all, identify a metric that objectively reflects the usage pattern. For all intents and purposes, traffic metrics seem to be the best choice. For a conclusive outcome, a minimum of a yearly record of at least one hour granularity of traffic sum is necessary.

All websites follow the 24-hour daily cycle from peak to trough. It is important to be aware of the exact times at which the system enters and leaves the periods of most intense activity. It is during that time that the system is most productive but at the same time most vulnerable. All maintenance work should be pushed out to the quieter trough periods.

In addition to a daily fluctuation, a weekly variance is observed. Weekend usage will probably differ from that of trading days. The pattern strongly depends on the nature of hosted content and cultural factors. For instance, websites with professional information are busiest during the week, while deals, movie streaming, and entertainment websites will be busier on weekends.

A *trend* is a long-term, gradual change of data point values, not influenced by seasonality and cyclical components. The quickest way to highlight its existence is to aggregate data points by week. Such improvised trend estimation satisfies most informal needs by hiding trading day effects. If you need exact trend estimation, export your data and use a statistical package capable of timeseries analysis.

Finally, long-term observations of traffic patterns reveal seasonal fluctuations caused by calendar events and holiday periods. Seasonal events occur around the same time every year. Some months of the year require more resources than others; in retail the first quarter of the year is known to be the quietest, while the final quarter the busiest due to the holiday season.

## CHAPTER 3

Alerting

Some people believe that alerting is an art for which proficiency takes long years of trial and error. Perhaps, but most of us can't wait that long. I prefer to view alerting as an exact science based on logic and probability. It's about balancing two conflicting objectives: *sensitivity*, or when to classify an anomaly as problematic, and *specificity*, or when is it safe to assume that no problem exists. These objectives pull your alerting configuration in two opposite directions. Figuring out the right strategy is not a trivial task, but its effectiveness can be measured. The right choice depends on organizational priorities, the level of recovery built into the monitored system, and the expected impact when things go awry. At any rate, there is nothing supernatural about the process; getting it right is well within everyone's reach.

The Challenge

In my experience, it's simply impossible to maintain focused attention on a timeseries in anticipation of a problem. The vast amount of information running through the system generates a great number of timeseries to watch. Hiring people solely for the purpose of watching performance graphs is not very cost effective, and it wouldn't be a very rewarding job either. Even if it was, though, I'm still not convinced that a human operator would be better at recognizing alertable patterns than a machine.

The process of alerting is full of unstable variables of a qualitative nature, and it presumes an element of responsibility. Priorities are open to interpretation, but the level of severity usually depends on what's at stake. The extent of pressure involved in incident response varies from organization to organization, but the overall process has a common pattern.

The goal of alerting is to draw operators' attention to noticeable performance degradation, which manifests itself in three general ways:

- Decreased quality of output
- Increased response time
- Loss of availability

The onus on the operator who receives an alert is to respond to it in a timeframe appropriate to the severity of the degradation. His task is to isolate and identify the source of the problem and mitigate the impact in the shortest time possible. The challenge of balancing sensitivity and specificity is to alert as soon as possible without raising false alarms.

Prerequisites

Effective alerting is more than creating alarms and sending notifications. It should facilitate the human response to mechanical faults and drive continuous improvement. To meet these goals, alerting requires a few basic components of IT infrastructure, without which a mature organization simply cannot exist.

Monitoring and Alerting Platform

First and foremost, you need a monitoring platform that meets a few conditions: it must have a well supported and easily definable way to deploy data gathering agents; it should have a flexible, feature-rich plotting engine that allows for graphing multiple timeseries on a single chart; and it must include an alerting engine that can support sophisticated alarm configurations (tens of thousands of alarms, aggregation, and suppression).

This book does not help you deploy a monitoring platform; I assume you already have one. If you don't and are wondering which monitoring system best addresses your needs, I recommend making an informed decision by consulting the following Wikipedia article (*http://bit.ly/RUbrWW*), mentioned earlier in Chapter 1.

Audit Trail

A lot of issues result from the fallout of planned production changes. Some of them may be executed automatically, such as a periodic rollout of security patches. Others are manual, like configuration changes carried out by an operator through step-by-step instructions. Maintaining an accurate and complete audit trail—a chronological record of changes in the system—helps in pinpointing cause and effect by letting you correlate aberrant system behavior with the times in the event log. A quick discovery of faults in this way significantly boosts the process of recovery.

Issue Tracking

An issue tracking system (ITS) helps prioritize reported alerts and thus helps you track the progress of issues as they are being resolved. Tickets coordinate collaboration between resolvers and ensure that the ball does not get dropped, so each and every alert should be recorded in an ITS. With it, the effectiveness of alerting can be reliably measured over time. This helpful side effect of an ITS helps in driving higher standards.

Understanding Failure and Its Impact

Maintaining a robust alerting configuration starts with realizing the cost of failure and the significance of reacting in time. The cost can be understood and expressed in a variety of ways: time, money, effort, quality, prestige, trust. Each organization can come up with its own definition. The bottom line is that each failure incurs costs corresponding to the extent of the failure's impact. The first step on the way to effective alerting is to come up with clear range of significance in order to set the priorities right.

Establishing Significance

Among many failures experienced in a daily system operation, only a fraction deserve an operator's attention.

Failures are eligible for alerts when their significance is high enough to negatively affect the system's operation. They are significant if the system will not recover from them by itself. Therefore, the severity of a failure can be considered in terms of two properties: recoverability and impact. Let's consider those two for a moment.

Recoverability is the potential of a system to restore its state to the prefailure mode without operator intervention. Recoverability can be imagined as a score combining the likelihood of a given failure to go away and the time necessary for its cessation.

Impact is the negative effect on the system's operation, reflected in the level of resource utilization as well as end user experience. It can be described as an unanticipated cost, which comes in various orders of magnitude. To quote just a few examples for an ecommerce website, from most to least severe:

Downtime
    People can't buy stuff, leading to loss of immediate revenue as well as potential future customers.

Partial loss of availability
    A fraction of customers won't spend their money on your site.

Increased response times
    Some users will get impatient and go off to the competition.

Decrease in content quality
People are less likely to remain on the site and therefore purchase stuff.

Suboptimal utilization of resources
This uses up money that can potentially be spent better.

Let's stagger recoverability and impact into three levels each, as depicted on Figure 3-1, to describe the severity of undesired events. The matrix illustrates a classification of events into nine separate bins, from most to least severe.

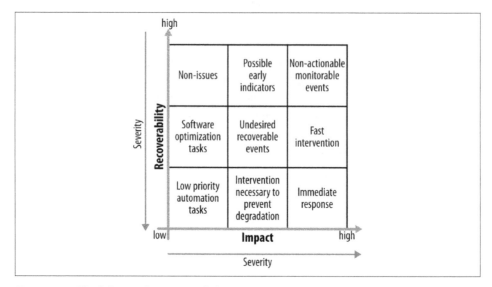

Figure 3-1. Eligibility and severity of alarming

1. Critical

   Sudden events with impact so severe as to block user access or severely impair the system's operation. A failure to prevent critical events increases system downtime and directly translates to unrecoverable losses in productivity or revenue.

2. Urgent

   Events when partial loss of availability is observed, when a fraction of users is unable to get onto the system, or a significant portion of the system becomes unresponsive. These kinds of events require fast intervention to minimize their impact and prevent them from escalating into critical events.

3. Intervention necessary

   Events that require intervention to prevent them from intensifying into critical events. They are not immediately catastrophic, but the system is at a high risk of collapsing without treatment. For instance, the system may build up a backlog that leads to processing delays.

4. Recoverable

   Negative events with relatively noncritical effect on the system, but with the potential to develop into bigger problems if not recovered within an expected timeframe. For instance, the failure of a background map-reduce job may be noncritical to the system's operation, and no alarm is necessary if a subsequent job succeeds.

5. Inactionable

   A group of events in which a small fraction of users faces transient but serious failures that immediately disappear by themselves. Because of the high speed of recoverability, the inactionable events get resolved before an operator could respond, so it would be ineffective to issue alerts for them. The frequency of these inactionable events should, however, be occasionally verified to ensure that momentary performance degradation remains isolated and negligible.

6. Automation Tasks

   Faults not having an immediate impact on the system's operation but with a potential of being a supporting factor in other failures.

7. Early Indicators

   Transient events of small to moderate impact affecting a tiny fraction of users. They come as a result of momentary resource saturation and small bugs and may be early indicators of the inability of a system to handle stress.

8. Optimization Tasks

   Events bearing no effect on a system's functionality but causing inefficiencies in resource utilization that could be eliminated by architectural restructuring or software optimizations.

9. Nonissues

   Anomalies with no perceivable impact, observable as a part of any system operation, particularly at scale.

Only the first four groups require alerting, because only in those cases is the system actually at risk and only then should the operator intervene and alter the system's state.

For the four alertable groups, the alerting configuration is considered in terms of two contradictory goals: speed and accuracy of detection.

The alerts for critical events should trigger as soon as the initial symptoms of grave failure are present. Critical events require immediate intervention, so it's okay to trade off reliability of detection for precious time that could be spent on mitigative action. If a few false positives are generated in the process—so be it.

The second group of events, classified as urgent, also necessitate quick intervention, but their relatively higher incidence and lesser severity allow you to wait for additional data points before raising an alarm. The alert is still issued relatively early, but with higher confidence.

System issues for the which operator's intervention is necessary but does not have to be immediate allows for more liberal data collection times. Effectively, an alert should be issued only when the existence of the problem has been established with a high degree of certainty—when enough aberrant data points are recorded.

Similarly, recoverable events should not trigger alerts until it becomes apparent that their recovery would take too long or could evolve into more serious problems.

The remaining five groups do not require alerting, but some organizations might choose to issue alerts and create low priority tickets for the purposes of accounting and offline investigations. In general, it is enough that low impact events are monitored and occasionally investigated to verify whether their levels of impact remain negligible.

Identifying Causes

The multitude of possible causes for a failure can be generally classified into four groups:

Resource unavailability or saturation
> This is by far the most common problem in production systems. Network blips and resource saturation routinely cause increased response times. In extreme cases, they may be responsible for a complete denial of service. Events causing excessive resource consumption include:
>
> - Exceptionally high rates of input
> - Malicious attacks
> - Shutting down portions of the system for maintenance
> - A whole range of operator errors
>
> Often these causes gradually lead up to saturation, rather than creating it immediately, and they might be prevented if they are detected early enough in the process. Well-designed systems implement throttling mechanisms or other sorts of admission control to gracefully degrade under excess load, as opposed to failing slow and hard.

Software problems

Software faults are very common and range from bugs to architectural limitations, dependency problems, and much more. Software bugs are present everywhere, but their likelihood is greater under conditions of high complexity, premature releases, bad design, and poor quality control practices. Some bugs are reproducible under high load, whereas other shows up after long running times. Once identified, they can be fixed relatively fast through the deployment of a patched version.

Software problems won't go away by themselves, however, and so they should be dealt with as part of daily operation. When monitoring brings software faults to operators' attention, those operators should be empowered to take corrective action. To make mitigation effective, operators need a clear versioning scheme with rich deployment instrumentation to allow for software rollbacks and roll-forwards.

Misconfigurations

Misconfigurations are a special kind of operational human error. Configuration errors are difficult to detect programmatically. Unnoticed by humans, they are likely to pass formal QA tests as well (if QA testing is a part of the process). They result in unfortunate and unintended consequences and are quite often noticed by the users before a mitigative rollback action can be taken. A notable example would be a leading search engine marking all web results as malicious content. Configuration settings, just like software, should be version controlled to make it possible to roll them back to a steady state.

Hardware defects

Hardware defects occur less frequently than software bugs, but when they do occur they tend to be hard to isolate and costly to deal with. The difficulty lies with the physical nature of the fix. While hardware faults are observed to a lesser extent in moderate-sized systems, they tend to emerge at large scale in busy production environments and become the norm. Hardware faults can cause significant delays in operation or cause complete device shutdown. Some hardware faults can be detected through scanning for error messages in OS level logs, but they often don't manifest their existence explicitly. They do become visible while monitoring groups of machines where single hosts reveal aberrant behavior.

Anatomy of an Alarm

The core functionality of an alarm is to trigger on detection of abnormal timeseries behavior, but the alerting system should also support the aggregation and conditional suppression of alarms. Conceptually, all three kinds of functionality are the LEGO bricks for creating robust and sophisticated alerting configurations.

This section attempts to describe a practical model for alarm configuration. It introduces a level of abstraction that sits on top of the alerting system to simplify the work of planning and implementing alerting configurations. If this seems like overengineering a combination of a threshold and a notification, please bear with me! With help, operators can design the most sophisticated alerting configurations through the use of Boolean logic, keeping things simple at the same time.

Boolean Function

An alarm can be seen as a definition of a Boolean function. At any point in time, its evaluation returns one of two possible states: alert or clear. Let's assign them binary values of 1 and 0, respectively. When the result of an evaluation changes—when its value goes from 0 to 1 or from 0 to 1—we're dealing with an *alarm state transition*.

An alarm function describes a set of relations between an arbitrary number of inputs, which fall into three types: metric monitors, date/time evaluations, and other alarms. All three also evaluate to Boolean values of 1 or 0.

The alarm function is reevaluated when any of its input components changes state (Figure 3-2). Every time a recalculation of the state leads to a transition from 0 to 1, the predefined transition action may be triggered: an alert is sent, a ticket gets created, or both.

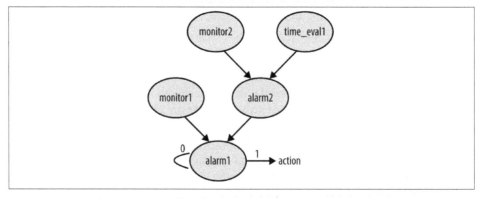

Figure 3-2. Representation of an alarm in the form of a binary decision diagram

In essence, an alarm can be defined as a shell encapsulating a condition and an action that will be triggered upon meeting the condition. That's the high level model—simple enough, right? Now, let me discuss its building blocks to justify the claim that it's so powerful as to allow for the creation of the most sophisticated configurations.

Metric Monitor

Metric monitors are the core of most alarms. They describe threshold breach conditions and transition their state when data points on the observed timeseries exceed or fall below expected limits. Metric monitors are made up of four parts:

- Name and dimensions of a metric, together with a summary statistic yielding a specific timeseries
- Threshold type and value
- Minimal duration of breach (number of data points for which the threshold must be crossed to trigger)
- Time necessary to clear (amount of time to wait until data points return to values within threshold, warranting a safe transition back into clear state)

It often happens that the monitored timeseries recovers after a single data point breach and such an event produces no or negligible impact. In order to avoid alarming on transient anomalies, a monitor defines the minimum number of data points required for transition into the alert state. Conversely, if the timeseries has been in breach for quite some time, a single healthy data point isn't necessarily an indication of recovery and shouldn't be a reason to immediately transition back into the clear state. For that reason, the monitor should also define the minimum number of healthy data points that warrant the return to clear state.

Typically, four threshold types are used: above, below, outside range, and data points that were not recorded.

Upper Limit. Upper limit threshold monitors trigger when data points exceed the pre-defined value. They are by far the most commonly used type of threshold. Whenever excessively high values on the underlying metric translate to increased costs or performance degradation, use the upper limit threshold monitor. This applies to metrics reporting resource consumption to warn about approaching utilization limits and to on-delay metrics to notify about extreme slowness.

Lower Limit. Lower limit threshold monitors trigger when metric levels fall below expected limits. They call the operator's attention to the depression in or absence of flow, events, or resource utilization. They are particularly useful for monitoring throughput metrics and are therefore extensively used in data pipelines. They are also a good fit for alarming on availability loss.

Outside Range. Range threshold monitors are used for timeseries whose data points are expected to oscillate within an area capped both under and above the threshold limits. They are useful for monitoring bidirectional deviations from a steady norm. An Outside Range monitor can be interpreted as a combination of two monitors defined by both an upper and lower limit condition, logically OR-ed together. By analogy, creation of an Inside Range monitor is possible too, but this one would find a lot fewer areas of application.

Most of the time, an Upper Limit threshold monitor will suit you better than its Outside Range counterpart. Just because a timeseries oscillates within a certain range doesn't mean that it is a good idea to use range-based thresholds. Consider, for example, a cache hit rate metric expressed in percentage terms: what percentage of web requests were served out of a Memcache server instead of a database? Let's assume that the values oscillate between 20% and 50%. If the value falls below 10% it might mean more load dispatched to the database directly, but if the upper limit is exceeded, there is no reason to worry: the caching server is doing its job, and this certainly is not a good reason for setting off an alarm.

Data Points Not Recorded. On some occasions a system may be down and thus stop recording any information. Technically, when no new data points arrive, neither the lower nor the upper limit threshold is breached, but it does not mean that the system is okay —quite the contrary. It is generally acceptable for a monitoring system to lag behind real-time data collection by one or two data points, but if more of them fail to show up on time, it might be a reason for investigation. This threshold type triggers on exactly that—it does not include a threshold value, just the maximum number of delayed data points that are considered an acceptable delay.

This threshold type can be used for monitoring irregular events with unpredictable running times. Think of software builds that run for hours. Suppose their build times vary from 3 to 10 hours, but they should never exceed 12 hours. Every time a build completes, a data point is uploaded to the metric with hourly granularity. A monitor that watches out for 12 empty data points could reliably report on suspiciously long running builds for which an absence of results warrants further investigation.

Time Evaluation

A time evaluation function defines a temporal condition that returns *true* at a specific point in time and *false* the rest of the time. There are many reasons why you'd want to include a time evaluation function as an input into your alarms. Let me list just a couple of examples:

- You want to suppress some group of alarms at a specific time of the day, when regular maintenance is carried out.
- You don't want the alarms to trigger actions on the weekends.

Time evaluation functions find their application mainly in the suppression of alarms, but they may also be used as an auxiliary trigger. For instance,

- If some metrics go beyond normal levels at specific times, due to the nature of your business, you may build an alarm that triggers when the metrics remain steady during expected peaks, and actually alarms on the absence of an anticipated event, or

- When you need to initiate an outage drill exercise, create an alarm that goes off on a certain day once a quarter, or

- You may simply wish to page the on-call engineer with a reminder about an upcoming event that requires extra vigilance.

Another Alarm as Input Source

Because alarm state evaluates to a Boolean, there is nothing preventing it from being an input to another alarm. Nesting alarms is a powerful concept that enables the creation of alarm hierarchies. Special attention must be paid to avoid circular dependencies, referring directly or indirectly to one's own value, possibly by a middle-man alarm; this makes no practical sense and therefore should be guarded against.

Suppression

You put alarms in place to eliminate the need for a human operator to continuously watch the system state. During scheduled maintenance, however, disruptions are expected and system metrics should be closely inspected at all times. The metrics are expected to display anomalies, and a planned outage should not trigger a storm of notifications that serve no purpose. It is therefore perfectly appropriate to momentarily suppress alarms that are known to trigger. To suppress an alarm means to prevent it from going off even when its threshold condition is breached.

Alarm suppression can be manual or automatic. Manual suppression should be enabled only for predefined periods of time, with an expectation that the alarms will be enabled automatically after the deadline is passed. This approach eliminates the danger that an operator might forget to unsuppress alarms after maintenance, which can potentially lead to prolonged dysfunction of the alerting setup.

In addition to manual control, the possibility of hands-off suppression opens the door for automation. Thanks to the Boolean evaluation of alarms, suppression is trivial to implement because a state of another monitor may be used as a Boolean input.

Let me explain this using an example. Suppose that two independent system components, A and B, exist on the same network. Each may fail for a number of independent reasons, so the two components are watched by two separate availability monitors.

When a monitor detects loss of availability, an alarm triggers and a ticket for the given component is created and placed in the operator's queue. One of the reasons for a failure may be the network link itself, which is also watched by a separate monitor. The alarm configuration for this system is summarized by the following table:

Alarm1 = ServiceA_Monitor

Alarm2 = ServiceB_Monitor

Alarm3 = Network_Monitor

When the network goes down, all three alarms go off and the operator receives three tickets for one issue. In most circumstances this is not desired.

In order to suppress generation of tickets and notifications for downstream elements of the system, event masking logic can be added. This is as simple as extending the condition of Alarm1 and Alarm2 by "AND NOT *SuppressionCondition*", to the following effect:

Alarm1 = (ServiceA_Monitor AND NOT Network_Monitor)

Alarm2 = (ServiceB_Monitor AND NOT Network_Monitor)

Alarm3 = Network_Monitor

This way, when the network fails the operator gets a single ticket of very high impact. If, after recovery of the network problem, any of the services is still out of balance and its state requires follow-up, appropriate tickets will get created automatically as soon as the network returns and renders the suppression rule inactive.

Aggregation

The third fundamental feature of alarming is aggregation, the ability to group related alarm inputs in order to de-duplicate the amount of resulting notifications.

Aggregation takes three basic forms:

Any

> The *Any* aggregation type means logically OR-ing inputs. This is the most sensitive type of aggregation and should be used when the monitored entity supports many critical components, each of which preferably has a low failure rate. The template for Any aggregation is:

> AnyAlarm = (Input1 OR Input2 OR Input3)

For an example where Any aggregation would be appropriate, think of a serial data pipeline, built of five components: A, B, C, D and E. Data enters at A and is processed sequentially until it leaves at E. If any single component or any combination of components fails, the pipeline stops. Therefore, logically OR-ing individual monitors always informs you about stoppage and produces only a single ticket.

All

The *All* type of aggregation consists of logically AND-ing all inputs. This very insensitive type of aggregation is used for higher order entities containing multiple noncritical subentities with a relatively high expected failure rate—in other words, when redundant components share work and one can take on the load of the others.

AllAlarm = (Input1 AND Input2 AND Input3)

As an example, imagine a tiny map-reduce cluster with three servers, each of which has a relatively high failure rate. Fortunately, over time and for the most part, the servers are capable of recovering by themselves. A single working machine in the cluster can handle number crunching on its own, even if it's a little slower than when it works with the other two. You want to alarm only when the continuity of work has been interrupted, that is, when all three servers experience failure at the same time. The solution is to aggregate all three monitors in an alarm through logical AND.

By Count

The *By Count* aggregation adds the result of Boolean evaluations (binary 1 and 0 values) from each of the inputs and tests the sum against the maximum allowable limit. So the following example allows at most one input to be in alarm at any given time, and sets off the alarm if two inputs evaluate to 1.

ByCountAlarm = ((Input1 + Input2 + Input3) >= 2)

As an example, suppose you have a bunch of hosts on which you monitor consumption of computational resources. You want to alarm as soon as the CPU utilization exceeds 60% on at least 30% of all machines, no matter how idle the remaining machines are. Assuming that you'd have a separate monitor for each host, the implementation in Python pseudocode would look as follows:

```
cpu_alarm = sum(cpu_monitor() for cpu_monitor in host_inputs) > len(host_inputs) * 0.30
```

Aggregation is as important for effective alerting as getting an accurate thresholds. When calculating how precise your alerting system is, duplicate tickets are seen as false alarms. Fortunately, aggregation opportunities are relatively easy to spot in the layout of the alarms structure. If you don't get it right at the start, that's fine, too. Getting enough duplicate alerts over time will nudge you to identify potential areas for improvement!

Case Study: A Data Pipeline

I'll use a concrete example to illustrate the applicability of the model in this chapter. Imagine a data pipeline composed of three serially connected components processing a stream of data: I will refer to them as loader, processor, and collector. For the pipeline to stay operational, the continuity of data flow must be kept up at all times for each component. If any one fails to process inputs, the pipeline stops. All three components record a flow metric with number of processed items per interval.

In the simplest scenario, a single monitor is created for each component, watching its respective flow metric. The condition on all monitors is set to trigger when the number of processed items falls below the threshold of one—in other words, when the data flow stops. The monitors are aggregated in a single alarm via the Any aggregation type. Thus, the failure of any one of the components corresponds to the stoppage of the entire pipeline. When the alarm triggers, an alert is issued to the operator.

Suppose that an empty pseudo-alarm has been created for signaling when the system is in maintenance mode. The pseudo-alarm is put into the alert state for the duration of a planned outage, whenever it takes place. This way, triggering the pipeline alarm can be prevented during maintenance by use the pseudo-alarm as a suppression rule. See Figure 3-3.

Now let me add a twist to the story. Suppose the pipeline is run by a large company that has adapted the *Service Oriented Architecture* (SOA) model, with each component being a separate service. The services are supported by independent teams, and the jurisdiction of every team ends at the borders of their service entry. In this case, a more precise alerting configuration might be required, as a failure of a single pipeline component should not be the reason for engaging everyone in resolution of the issue. Three separate alarms, each containing its own monitor, should be created to watch the pipeline with a service-level granularity.

Additionally, the definition of service failure should also be clarified here: the service experiences failure if it stops processing inputs—provided that the inputs are still being sent by the upstream component. If the component doesn't process inputs because it hasn't received any, then it's not really at fault. This exception can be implemented by expanding the suppressing condition by the monitor of the upstream service. See Figure 3-4.

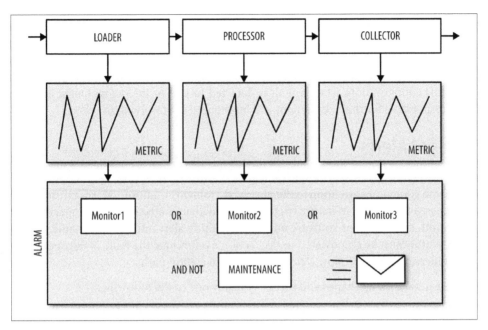

Figure 3-3. Simple alarm aggregating all pipeline components

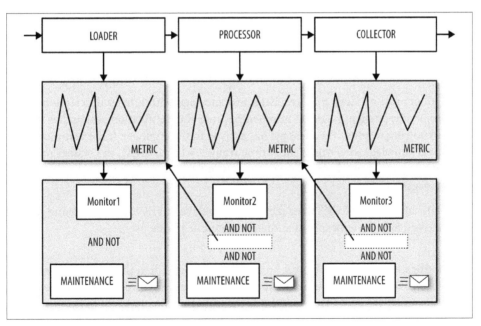

Figure 3-4. Separate alarms for each respective components with suppression when up-stream problems are detected

By using a monitor of the upstream service as a suppression, downstream teams avoid receiving inactionable alerts. Although, technically, both an alarm and a monitor could be used for suppression, it makes functional sense only to use the latter. Only the monitor truly reflects the operational state of the upstream service and, unlike an alarm, its state cannot be suppressed. It does, therefore, reliably inform about upstream service health. With this configuration, when a fault is detected in one of the components, only the team responsible for that component will be engaged for resolving the issue.

Types of Alerts

When an alarm goes off and transitions into the alert state, it may send a notification to draw the operator's attention to the observed problem condition. Alarm notifications are referred to as *alerts*. Whether triggered by a malicious attacker, a bad capacity plan, bandwidth saturation, or software bugs, the resulting alert must be actionable, that is, the operator must be empowered to take action to eliminate the fault. If the operator is out of ideas, he should follow a clearly defined escalation path.

Alerts can take many shapes and forms, typically one of the following:

Email

> The most common form of notification is an email message, due to lack of associated costs, wide distribution, and high reliability of timely delivery.

> Email is normally used as an auxiliary notification medium, because being so abundant in our lives as it is today, it is likely to get ignored. In addition to that, at present, GSM coverage is more widespread than Internet access, which is why SMS and a cellular phone based notification process is considered more reliable.

SMS

> An operator on duty may receive a text message with a brief description of the problem referencing a ticket number. Because the notification system has no way of knowing whether the message has arrived to the engineer, if the text message is not acknowledged within a short time frame (5-15 minutes), the system proceeds with automatic escalation to higher levels of support and often all the way up the management chain.

> Main advantages of SMS messages include their relatively low cost, fast and reliable delivery, and the widespread audience of mobile phone users.

Phone call

> Notification by phone involves an automated voice call to the on-duty engineer. It requires immediate status confirmation and usually involves making some sort of decision on the spot. The operator is presented with a choice of options to which she may respond through dialing assigned action keys, such as

1 - Acknowledgment

3 - Escalation to higher level support

9 - Resolution of the issue

The biggest advantage of alerting via voice call is that it experiences virtually no response waiting time. If the responsible party does not take the call, the escalation path may be followed immediately. Receiving an automated voice call takes on average between 15 seconds and 1 minute. Although getting a large number of SMS messages at once is tolerable, prioritizing a large number of phone calls might be more challenging.

Miscellaneous notifications
Sound and flashing lights are an alternative way to catch an operator's attention. This kind of alert is rarely used (outside of Hollywood), due to lack of durability (there is no sign that the alert happened) and dubious deliverability (the operator might have been asleep while the light was flashing).

All production alerts should be recorded in an ITS as tickets. That way, you're not letting anything slip and you're generating meta information about the alerting process that can later be measured and used to institute alerting improvements.

Setting Up Alarms

Setting up alarms is a four-step process. It involves identifying threatening behavior, establishing its significance, expressing that in terms of alerting goals, and implementing alarm configuration along with suppression and aggregation.

Identifying Impact

The process begins with realizing what the problems actually are. At the beginning of the chapter I listed the three main failure groups: decreased quality of output, increased response time, and loss of availability. While this short list is universal, it isn't necessarily exhaustive, and specialized systems might consider other types of issues threatening. If that's the case with your system, it's important to realize what the issues are.

Next, you must find out how problems are manifested through timeseries. What metrics reveal the information you need? How are the symptoms measured? What are the bottlenecks? What kind of system behavior exacerbates these bottlenecks? If it turns out that system metrics do not reliably indicate the issues, you might need to deploy an external measurement source.

Availability is expressed as the percentage of time the system responds as expected. It is measured through proactive probes issued at evenly spaced time intervals. When the system does not reply with a pre-agreed response within an acceptable time delay, loss of availability is assumed. Internal health probes are helpful to offer evidence of system state internally, but remember that availability can be measured reliably only from external probes. It's always a good idea to have both internal and external monitoring in place.

When loss of availability is partial—affecting only a selected group of users—and does not manifest itself immediately through failed health probes, it is also possible to notice it from traffic levels that are running below forecast. This approach is less conclusive because there might be many reasons for reduced traffic levels (such as an important national sporting event), but it is still very reliable.

There is typically no single answer to what causes high response times, but a shortage of an underlying resource is involved most of the time, be it network bandwidth, CPU, I/O, or RAM. Keeping a close eye on these resources ensures fast and conclusive incident response. It is important to note that requests with extremely long response times have the same effect as loss of availability: impatient users will simply give up. At the same time, long running requests still take up resources that could be used better by successful requests.

Degradation in the quality of output is hardest to define. It depends ultimately on the system's purpose and is inherently subjective. But it is not impossible to measure! If your system has users, try to draw conclusions from their behavior—your customers value their time and recognize quality, especially when you have them pay for it.

Establishing Severity

Alarms are set off in response to fluctuations of data points on timeseries. Some value changes are a clear-cut indication of existing trouble, whereas other reveal early symptoms of potential risk, but they all can be assigned a meaning: a suspected impact and its matching severity. Establishing severity is crucial for the effective prioritization of issues coming in as tickets. Figure 3-5 suggests an assignment of severity based on impact and recoverability factors based on the categories in "Establishing Significance" (page 49).

The following list is a suggested assignment of priorities to types of incidents, ranging from highest to lowest priority:

1. System downtime
2. Partial loss of availability, severe performance degradation
3. Quality loss
4. Multisecond availability loss events, hard drives reaching 90% of used space
5. Minimal rates of errors observed over long periods, frequent CPU utilization spikes

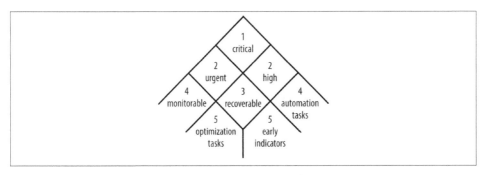

Figure 3-5. Assignment of alarm severity to event significance

Picking the Right Timeseries

Next, it's time to select one metric, among the many candidates, that is best capable of meeting your monitoring objectives. Chapter 2 described metrics in terms of their properties. The classification can be used to answer questions regarding suitability: What type of metric is best to alarm on throughput limits? If I want to alarm on availability, is a metric generated by an internal source a good enough indicator? Will a passive or active approach be more conclusive for my purpose? If I want to alarm on high percentiles, will a single-N metric give me what I want?

Once the metric is selected, you must choose a summary statistic to generate a timeseries to monitor. The statistic should reflect your alerting goals. Stats can be divided by applicability as follows:

- *n*, sum: good fit for measuring the rate of inflow and outflow, such as traffic levels, revenue stream, ad clicks, items processed, etc.

- Average, median (*p50*): suitable for monitoring a measurement of center. Timeseries generated from these statistics give a feel for what the common performance level is and reliably illustrate its sudden changes. When components and processes have a fair degree of recoverability, an average is preferred to percentiles. When looking for most typical input in the population, the median is preferred to the average.

- High and low percentiles: suited to monitoring failures that require immediate intervention. The extreme percentiles of the input distribution can reveal potential bottlenecks early, through making observations about small populations for which performance has degraded drastically. For speedy detection of faults, percentiles are preferred to the average because extreme percentile values deviate from their baseline more readily and thus cross the threshold sooner.

Percentiles of input distribution are always presented in ascending order. When using them, you must know whether you're interested in numbers at the beginning or at the end of the distribution. Let me illustrate this through an example: when setting alarms around latency it is appropriate to watch high percentiles, such as *p95* or *p99*, because the smaller the value the better, while alarming on dips of revenue inflow would require watching low percentiles, such as *p1* or *p10*.

Most monitors are set up to inform about exceeding a limit (Upper Limit threshold crossed), which is why the use of high percentiles is more widespread.

 It's not a good idea to set up monitors around *p0* and *p100*. They catch just the extreme values, which are not necessarily indicative of a problem. Setting up alarms to alert on outliers guarantees queue noise, confusion and, in the long term, frustration. It's okay to use *p99* if your sample set is large enough, approximately 100 samples. Internet giants can reliably detect impact changes at *p99.9* or even *p99.99*, but not on *p100*.

In practice, the selection of a summary statistic applies only to multi-N metrics. Single-N metrics have one data input per data point, so every summary statistic produces the same value, except for *n*, which is always equal to 1 (a single input per data point).

Configuring Monitors

Metric monitors are at the heart of most alarms. A monitor is attached to a timeseries and evaluates a small set of recent data points against a predefined threshold condition to detect and report a breach. To communicate the alert and clear states, it includes three pieces of information: timeseries, threshold, and number of data points in the threshold breach.

Coming Up with a Threshold

Threshold values carry a meaning. The threshold separates the normal from the potentially unhealthy state that might require intervention. This section discusses how to come up with values for two types of thresholds: *constant or static thresholds*, for which values can be established independently of the reported inputs, and *data-driven thresholds*, which derive their values from historical data points on timeseries.

Static thresholds. On many occasions, the value for a threshold may be predetermined through prior analysis. Such thresholds are referred to as static ones. They do not require readjustments over time. Let's have a look at a couple of examples.

By predetermined I do not mean as agreed by the SLA—beware of SLA-driven thresholds. The point of setting up alarms is to facilitate timely response to a production issue in order to avoid or minimize SLA breaches. When an alert is sent on an SLA breach, it's already too late.

Utilization limit

Utilization limits that represent a threat can be determined through stress testing or by observing performance under production load. When severe performance degradation can be tracked back to a utilization level of a particular resource, its value at the point at which the degradation began should be recorded and used as a threshold. Static utilization thresholds can be applied to all sorts of resources, such as storage space, memory, and IOPS.

Discontinuation of flow

Flow continuity has special significance in data pipelines. Any disruption of operation may lead to an accumulation of potentially unrecoverable backlog.

Suppose data is processed in a pipeline at a certain rate. Recording a flow metric with the number of processed items produces a timeseries with non-zero values during pipeline operation. It flattens out at zero when the pipeline isn't operational. With that, setting up a threshold condition as "below 1" reliably informs about discontinuation of processing. Alarming at zero is a valid but extreme case. The threshold may, of course, be set accordingly to a low nonzero value if a minimum viable throughput rate is estimated (or established empirically during an outage).

Loss of availability

Availability metrics can be interpreted as expressing coverage of availability, and as such they are presented in percentage terms. Ideally, availability should be maintained at 100% at all times, so any episode of loss falling below three nines (99.9%) in a measured interval might be a reason for investigation, depending on the scale of operation and the impact resulting from loss. At any rate, availability metrics are good candidates for a constant threshold ranging somewhere between 99% and 100%.

Data-driven thresholds. For timeseries with evolving patterns, thresholds should be calibrated to reflect their most recent state. Data-driven thresholds require periodic readjustment. This approach emphasizes the importance of monitoring as a process and yields high rates of accuracy. Having said that, it comes at an expense of added complexity. The method to use for threshold calculations depends on the underlying pattern of a given timeseries and may vary, but the most important thing is to anchor threshold values to real data.

Here I'll describe a model that I've used to successfully drive up precision and recall of alerting configurations in a busy production environment. If you're looking to set up alarms on timeseries that evolve from week to week, it will probably be the right choice for you, too. It has been proved to work with a wide range of patterns, including *p99* of network latency, error rates, traffic bursts, and data queue levels on thousands of alarms in a large-scale production system.

Distribution of Data Inputs and Data Points

Percentile distribution can be analyzed on any set of numbers. This book refers mostly to distribution of data inputs per data point. In this section, however, I talk a lot about percentiles of historical data point values. It's important to keep these two apart, so just to recap:

- Multi-N metrics produce timeseries whose data points are built of multiple data inputs. Data inputs that construct each data point can be analyzed in terms of their percentile distribution. In other words, data inputs in each time interval are sorted and assigned a rank from 0 to 100, as described in Chapter 2. That way you can plot a timeseries of, say, *p99* of response times, which can generate a chart of the slowest 1% of the responses.

- A range of data point values on the resulting timeseries may also be interpreted in terms of their percentile distribution. For the remainder of this section, I will refer to percentile distribution of data points on a timeseries, as opposed to data inputs making up a data point.

The idea behind the calculation model is a simple one: look at recent historical timeseries and try to identify alertable data points. Depending on the context and type of metric, these will have either extremely high or atypically low values. Let's assume we're looking for high values, since this is the use case most of the time.

Suppose you're looking at a timeseries representing error rates from a busy application server, as represented on the lefthand side of Figure 3-6. The metric is of flow *type* and the summary statistic used is *sum*. The metric is quite spiky, but most of the time the errors oscillate at a rate of 80 per data point. They hardly ever exceed the value of 250 per interval. The same data points arranged in percentile plot are shown on the corresponding image on the right side.

This metric was recorded in a healthy state; that is, no sustained error rate was observed. The few transient spikes reaching above 40 were short-lived and therefore inactionable.

Notice how the percentile distribution curve goes up steeply towards the end. Its value at the 97th percentile is 240. It means that 97% of the time, the error rate is less than 239 errors per interval, and 3% of the time, it's at 240 and more. It's easy to agree with these proportions when looking at the timeseries on the left.

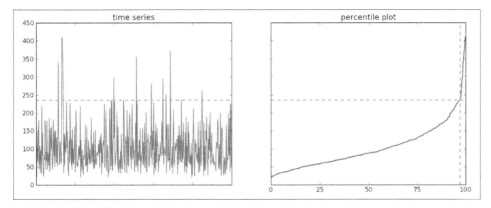

Figure 3-6. Timeseries and percentile plot of average response times

Let's see whether 240 makes a good threshold in this case. Suppose the timeseries interval is at one minute granularity. If the monitor is set to trigger on one data point, we'd get about 40 false alarms a day. Alarming on two consecutive data points elevated to a value of 240 ends up producing up to two false alarms per day, while three data points work out at a false alarm once a month. That's a reasonable speed-precision trade-off, but extending it further by one data point gives in effect an almost sure-fire indication of something going on.

Sounds good, but we're left with two more problems:

- What if historical data registered a long lasting outage during which error rates were very high? The next recalibration will drive the threshold so high that it will become insensitive to any and all problems.

- What if the error rate decreases drastically over time? It would be annoying to have alarms trigger on two errors per data point, if *p97* goes down to a value of 1 some time in the future.

Both problems are worth consideration: you want monitors to evolve with the metric, but you also want to keep threshold values within reason.

The way to do that is to agree on the lower and upper monitor safety limits. You have to answer the following two questions: what's the highest possible error rate that will not be considered a problem? and at what value do I want the threshold to stop going higher? You can use your judgment, carry out an analysis on a larger data sample, or look for guidance in the SLA to answer these questions (but effectively alarm on values below SLA figures). That way you allow the threshold to self-adjust, but within the limits of common sense.

I first used this method to monitor 800 logical entities with diversified usage patterns. Error rates ranged from the average of 0 to 250 per data point. Manual estimation of proper thresholds was out of the question and silver-bullet thresholds (at around 200 errors) for all entities was inherently ineffective: some alarms never triggered, while others were constantly in alert. We monitored at *p97* of the past weeks' data, setting a global lower limit for all alarms at 50 and an upper limit at 350.

The calculation model can be formulated in terms of reproducible steps and implemented in a few lines of code in your favorite scripting language.

1. Determine what the lower and upper limits as well as the selected percentile should be.

2. Extract a week's worth of data points from the timeseries to monitor. If you use a one-minute interval, that should leave you with a list of 10080 numbers. For a five-minute interval it's 2016 numbers.

3. Sort them in ascending order. You're now able to select percentiles of data point distribution. The last item on the list corresponds to the largest data point: *p100*. Every other percentile must be selected by rank. For the purpose of this exercise, the following formula for calculating the rank should do:

   $$n\text{th percentile rank} = (n * \text{number of data points}) / 100$$

4. Round the resulting number to the next integer and select the value at the *n*th percentile rank as your threshold.

5. If the value exceeds the upper limit or falls below the lower limit, disregard the value and choose the respective limit instead.

Example 3-1 is a simple implementation of the process in Python.

Example 3-1. Function assisting in selection of a percentile threshold.

```python
def get_threshold(datapoints, percentile=97, lower=None, upper=None):
    """Calculate a percentile based threshold."""
    sorted_points = sorted(datapoints)
    if percentile == 100:
        return sorted_points[-1]
    perc_value = sorted_points[percentile*len(datapoints)/100]
    if perc_value < lower:
        return lower
    elif perc_value > upper:
        return upper
    return perc_value
```

This calculation method is just an example. You could probably come up with another one that's better suited to your use case. For instance, you could set the threshold at three standard deviations above the average of all data points for a timeseries with a steady baseline, or you could pull out the median (*p50*) and set the threshold at two times its value on a fluctuating stock metric.

If you have no idea which model would be best, though, the method I've presented definitely makes a good start. Here are some reasons why:

- It can be applied to sparse metrics (those that happen to report no data in certain intervals).
- It does not require a normal distribution of data points or of differences in their values.
- It does not require timeseries to have a baseline.
- It puts emphasis on peaks in metrics following cyclic patterns,
- It can be applied to stock, flow, and throughput metrics with the same level of validity based on the "percentage of time" limit.

Breach and Clear Delay

The selection of breach and clear delay is almost as important as accurate threshold estimation.

Selecting the number of data points to alarm should reflect alerting goals. For critical and urgent issues it makes sense to alarm as early as possible, because quick response in these cases is vital. For less urgent and recoverable issues, it's okay to wait a little longer, because these are unlikely to immediately catch the operator's attention anyway. Letting a few more data points arrive raises the confidence level that something important is happening and improves precision.

The question is how to set off alarms as soon as possible, but not too soon. Unfortunately, it's hard to get an easy answer along these lines, and the objectives will have to be balanced. The sooner the alarm comes, the more likely it's just an anomaly. Of course, with issues of high criticality it is better to be safe than sorry, but too many false positives lead to desensitization in operators, which has some serious adverse effects.

The following table is a recommendation for an allocation of the monitor's breach delay, based on my experience of working in ops teams.

Severity	Breach Duration (minutes)	Example
Super-critical	1-2	Shutdown, high visibility outage
Critical, high priority	3-5	Partial loss of availability, high latency
Medium, normal	6-10	Approaching resource saturation
Low priority and recoverable	11 and beyond	Failed back-end build

Setting Up Alarms

In the final stage, the alerting configuration is implemented by putting all pieces of the puzzle together: the monitors, alerting configuration, aggregation, and suppression.

An average alarm consists of one or more monitors aggregated in some fashion and a notification action that is triggered by alarm's state transition.

The alert takes one or more forms. It's common to send out an email and a text message. If the alarming engine interfaces with the ITS, the alarm may also define a ticket to be filed.

It's always a good idea to track all alertable production issues through tickets. Sometimes, the alarm evaluation engine plugs directly into an ITS, which takes over alerting functionality with support for following escalation paths.

When including ticket definitions in an alarm, it's a good idea to follow a few simple guidelines:

- Set severity accordingly. It's tempting to assign higher urgency to a group of tickets just to have people pay more attention to them. But if it's not justified, operators will notice and start to ignore such tickets, and this will have adverse effects on the quality of work in the long run.

- Put specific symptoms in ticket's title. "Slow response times" is less informative than "Response times p99 exceeded 3 seconds for 3 data points." Do not include suspected causes in the description or you're going to have your colleagues chase red herrings.

- Place hints or a checklist in the description that outlines where to look for answers. Not everyone is an expert in every type of problem and you won't want to leave the newcoming members of the team behind.

Testing Alerting Configurations

In order to verify the faultlessness of your alarm configuration, you can perform a quick "smoke test." The idea is to trick the alarms into thinking that a production system is at risk, but without really exposing it to any.

A good way to go about this is to attempt to fool the data collection agent by providing it with false source information. For log reading and scanning agents, that means pointing the agent at forged logs containing alertable data inputs. Simply injecting error messages or replacing healthy logs with the forged ones should suffice.

It is somewhat harder to verify the correctness of health check probers or interface readers, because they may be pointing at hardcoded destinations. If there is no other way to fool the agent to report the arranged fault and you have access to its source code, running a modified agent to see the results might still be OK.

This way you verify whether your monitoring system reports data inputs as expected and whether the alarms responded to it accordingly. As a measure of last resort, you may choose to manually inject data inputs into your metrics, imitating an agent. This verifies the alarm setup, provided that the agent reports the inputs the same way.

Alerting Suggestions

Chapter 2 talked about monitoring coverage and suggested metrics that ought to be gathered for purposes of monitoring. However, not all metrics should have alarms set up against them. The following minimalist list offers practical suggestions for metrics worth considering as candidates for alerting. Those metrics were used in production systems I worked with. Your system might have different usage patterns, or you might be responsible just for its small parts and won't necessarily alert on all layers in the solution stack. You might be running a throughput intensive application and need to pay closer attention to I/O metrics. Whatever your business needs may be, try to operate according to the principle of monitoring extensively and alerting selectively: identify what metrics drive your business and work top-down to set up alarms around timeseries behind key performance indicators.

1. Resources

   Network latency and packet loss
   > Ping an external and an internal location a couple of times every minute. Record the round-trip time for the latency metric, along with 0 if the packet returned successfully and 1 otherwise as a packet loss metric. The average will return packet loss in percentage terms.

   CPU utilization
   > CPU utilization is a great universal indicator of computational strain. On Linux, parse */proc/stat* or have the System Activity Reporter (SAR) interpret it for you.

   Available disk space and memory
   > Prevent local storage from filling up and monitor for the amount of free space approaching limits. If you can't do this reliably, you should alert on it. Using up local storage space might induce unpredictable behavior in your application.

2. Platform

Turnaround times

Extract and upload response time statistics from application or middleware logs. Monitor changes in average and percentiles deep in the tail (*p99*).

Response codes

In a web application, record error HTTP response codes. Alarm on unusual proportions of bad requests and server problems.

3. Application

Availability

Set up external health checks from multiple locations and issue a test request once a minute. Record 1 on success and 0 on failure and alarm when the average falls below 99% (0.99) or whatever your SLA dictates.

Error rate

Define what constitutes usage errors and monitor them closely. Alarm when errors reach relatively high proportions.

Content freshness

If your application delivers evolving content, measure its freshness. Record an age metric (the difference in seconds between now and last content update) and alarm when the number of seconds approaches SLA deadline.

## CHAPTER 4

At Scale

Scale invites complexity. Complexity breeds confusion. Confusion, in turn, increases the likelihood of error. Even more mistakes are made under pressure resulting from deadlines, the time-critical nature of the business, or high external visibility. Timely response to production issues becomes more difficult at scale.

Some amount of complexity is unavoidable, so striving for simplicity, while a good thing in itself, is not the same as achieving it. Likewise, working under pressure is not something that will go away anytime soon. When is the right time to expand the team? Then again, the more people on the team, the harder it is to maintain consistency.

Increasing a system's manageability is a sure way to counter these factors. Rich instrumentation is a necessary yet not sufficient condition. If your system is expanding, this chapter might help you in planning an alerting configuration that scales along with it. If you have already reached the critical mass and monitoring is starting to become increasingly more complicated, this chapter will help you get back on track. It describes best practices for developing managed alerting configurations.

Implications of Scale

Large-scale information systems consist of numerous groups of interconnected computers. Their numbers start in the region of hundreds and go beyond tens of thousands. To improve resilience, availability, and access times, the systems may be distributed in diverse locations across the world. The computers communicate over a best-effort network, reliability of which cannot be taken for granted. The more complex hardware pieces the system consists of, the higher the possibility of failure in one of the individual parts. At a large scale, failure is not unusual.

Operating large systems comes at a cost. Their operation typically provides an important service and generates significant revenue streams. Any moment of downtime brings down the service and translates to losses. This makes failures in big systems highly visible, not only within the organization that runs them, but also in the media if the system provides a popular public service.

It is for that reason that organizations operating at large scale put great emphasis on preventative measures. They can include investigations into anomalies and atypical usage patterns aimed at ruling out any possibility of problem escalation. In low-visibility organizations, on the other hand, it is somewhat acceptable to respond to alerting events in a reactive rather than proactive way. It is also permissible in small settings to close up shop for an upgrade and ask users to come back later. The same is not an option in big systems. They require staggered, continuous maintenance, carefully carried out in phases.

Information systems process and store data to extract specific meanings. Raw data enter the system with various, sometimes unpredictable frequencies and the outcome of processing takes different forms. Processed data may be volatile and lose validity within minutes, as in the case of short-lived stock market price projections or relevance suggestions on a social networking site. Other processed data may be long-lived and relatively bulky to store, such as video clips on a broadcasting website. A system's architecture is shaped by existence and values of many such values, including data volatility and the cost of retention.

The designer makes a series of trade-offs, giving up efficient utilization of one resource in order to accommodate better utilization of a more essential resource. As a result, specific purpose systems are well suited for solving one kind of a problem but not the other—and some of their components will always be more prone to failure than others. An overall calculation of a system's durability should put the most weight on the durability of its weakest link.

In busy production environments with data processing rates of terabytes per second, the Law of Large Numbers applies. This makes their monitoring a great learning opportunity. Data generated at such magnitude of scale approximates mathematical models very closely and assumptions can be made with higher confidence. On the other hand, even small changes, assumed to cause disruption at seemingly negligible levels, might affect thousands of users. Even small mistakes can become highly visible. Finding out about faults from your users is never a good place to be. This is yet another reason for special care in carrying out daily operations and the need for fine-grained monitoring.

Finally, delays tell the story. Increased network latencies and system response times indicate overall performance degradation. Time delays can be seen as the most universal currency of performance. Small increases in response times might be an indication of increased load, but when delays rise to exceptionally high levels, they become a serious problem. Users tend to respond immediately by demonstrating their lack of patience. Internet giants are extremely sensitive to latency because it directly affects their bottom line.

Less pronounced shifts in delay time patterns might not always have a direct impact, but they do point to potentially worrisome changes downstream in the solution stack. Big systems supply enough inputs to reliably detect subtle changes. Detecting and dealing with them remains a focus of operations at scale.

Considering these aspects of large systems, a set of assumptions about the operation of large-scale systems can be drawn.

- Data enters and leaves with varying intensity and frequency, both of which are subject to a high degree of unpredictability.
- The scale of operation necessitates continuous maintenance.
- Increases in response time and latency adds costs to the organization.
- The longer the component interdependency chain is, the higher the likelihood of hitting a bottleneck.
- Failures are inevitable; they are the norm. The aim is to minimize their effects.

Composition of Large-Scale Systems

Data flow in a system is often compared to fluid conveyance in a set of pipes. The data is encapsulated in the form of messages and continuously passes through the system. Large information systems are composed of subsystems made up of components, which in turn are subdivided. The requests are routed between components according to some application logic. Components in each subsystem take different functional shapes, including but not limited to the following:

Service interface
> The way to take in and serve data, most frequently in the form of requests and responses. Interfaces can be read-write to allow submission of data, or read-only, meant exclusively for data consumption. Present day services are commonly built on top of a well defined HTTP interface.

Data processor
> Software that extracts selected aspects of information from the data and presents it in an alternative, usually more compact form. Processors may be real-time or offline, for example, a search result rank calculator or a map-reduce cluster.

Data pipeline

A serial chain of specialized data processors and transformers, taking a data stream at the ingress and returning it processed at the egress. Pipelines are built with continuity of data processing in mind and their end-to-end latency of processing is optimized to be as short as possible.

Datastore

A repository of data objects designed for specific access and persistence patterns. Examples include databases, network filesystems, shared storage systems, and cache fleets.

In order to meet the load and provide basic redundancy, the components are deployed to groups of hosts, or server fleets. Placing any of the components on a single server creates a *Single Point of Failure* (SPoF) because a failure of a single machine can be responsible for an entire system stopping its functionality and postponing operation. SPoFs must, therefore, be avoided.

The components of an application may be loosely or tightly coupled; the service interface and data processor may operate as separate fleets of hosts, but it is not uncommon to see them run out of the same server. Decoupling helps isolate failures, but introduces additional cost and overhead in data transmission. Each component is a computational platform consisting of a hardware and software stack. If components are coupled, it means that they share a portion of the platform at least up to the operating system layer. This has important implications for fault finding: an intensive utilization of resources by one component might slow down another.

A system in distributed operation is a bunch of computers collaborating on the network. While the computers are not necessarily plugged into each other in any particular order, a system's logical architecture does depend on how the data is processed, the frequencies at which it enters and leaves the system, and in what form. Some systems crunch big data sets, others are expected to produce meaningful result in real-time, and yet others are developed with persistence in mind to provide distributed storage for high-availability of data retrieval. Regardless of the purpose, a system's composition should be clearly defined in terms of its fundamental components, their coexistence, and architectural layout. Such a layout map serves as a base for establishing what areas should be covered by monitoring, and in case of failures it may serve as a reference guide for operators who are not familiar with the system intimately.

Commonalities of Large-Scale Alerting Configurations

Effective alerting configurations are rare. Most of them come with time, often built through trial and error. Interestingly though, they all share the same three characteristics: the thresholds are *cleanly ordered*, *data-driven*, and *reevaluated* when baselines shift. These rules apply to systems of any size, but their value becomes truly apparent in large and complex settings, where the system evolves, maintenance is laborious, and alarm thresholds are a moving target.

Order

Highly manageable large-scale systems are organized hierarchically and benefit extensively from the use of namespaces. Such a structured organization of alarms empowers the operators to work with alerts with more effectively.

Consistent namespacing allows for reliable audits and facilitates housekeeping. Alarms may be reliably classified as stale or obsolete if they don't reflect the current configuration or hierarchy of the system. Such alarms may subsequently get cleaned up to reduce their maintenance cost and prevent confusion among engineers. Additionally, order simplifies the task of setting up aggregation and suppression, and is a major factor behind alerting's effective manageability.

Data-Driven Organization

Timeseries data stores valuable information about the long-term process of change. This information should be used to drive alarm thresholds, as explained in "Data-driven thresholds" (page 67).

Threshold values, calculated from historical observations, anchor alarm behavior at real data. Some metrics produce continuous streams of data. These may oscillate around an almost constant value or be subject to seasonal cycles. Other metrics yield occasional spikes, not all of which indicate real issues. The baseline, the magnitude of failure, and the existence of anomalies should all be taken into account. A sound and reproducible calculation model leads to stronger detectability and reduction in human effort. The applicability of each calculation model is tied to the underlying data patterns, but they'll nearly always do a better job than a human.

Reevaluation

Many things will change over time, starting with hardware and infrastructure, through code efficiency, ending with traffic patterns. Although not all changes come at once, they will arrive eventually. In reality some changes are more progressive than others, and some configurations require a rich granular set of alarms while others do not. For that reason, different groups of alarms require reevaluation at different time intervals. When monitor thresholds are refreshed regularly to adjust to changes in usage patterns, alerting becomes significantly more sensitive and specific.

Monitoring Coverage

Large, manageable systems are organized in hierarchies, grouped by components and their relevant logical entities, according to the number of abstract dimensions that they operate in. The resulting software stack is then replicated to multiple locations around the world. In this context, a *dimension* is a way of presenting measurements that reflects the system's architecture and location. Full monitoring coverage should reflect as many dimensions as there are in the system.

Consider a simplistic model of a three-tier system expressed in terms of its dimensions, depicted in Figure 4-1.

- Dimension 1: covering each of the three tiers—the front end, the application layer, and the back end
- Dimension 2: vertically spanning the layers of hardware and solution stack
- Dimension 3: all server entities

Effective monitoring should cover all components of a system at its many levels of granularity. The operator must be able to get an immediate insight into parts of the system where faults are suspected, zoom in or out into arbitrary levels of data granularity, and overlay cross-layer metrics freely to highlight correlative relationships. You need to realize the kinds of structures shown in Figure 4-1 in order to make reliable assumptions.

Reflecting Dimensions in Metrics

Big systems with comprehensive monitoring collate millions of inputs into hundreds of thousands of data points per minute. Most of them will never get looked at. The penetration rate of metric data in large enterprises is estimated to be around 1%—and that's okay, because most of the monitoring data is collected just in case, for real-time inspection during an event response. In reality, only a small fraction of timeseries is constantly monitored by alarms and through dashboards and even fewer of them will be used for long-term analysis of seasonality trends.

When a need arises, the operator must know how to find her way through the remaining 99% of metrics in search of the defects. Data must be reported systematically. The question is how to report and store metrics so they can be retrieved with minimum effort and, in the process, discovered intuitively.

The way to do this is by storing the data so as to reflect a system's dimensions. In other words, every data input consists of a numeric value and a set of properties describing its origin and the circumstances under which the input was collected. All these properties can be seen as dimensions and their values can be interpreted as data addresses in an abstract multidimensional space. Through referencing data by their properties and origin, specific subsets of recorded inputs can be carved out from a metric and presented in the form of a timeseries.

Let me explain this idea by expanding a little on the example from Figure 4-1. Suppose we have three groups of hosts representing the front end, middleware, and the back end.

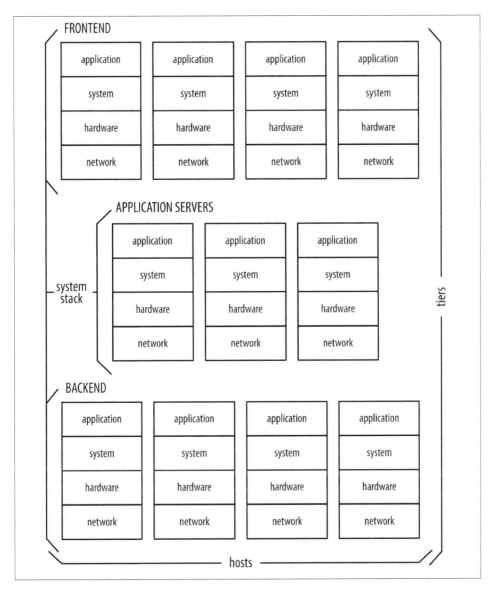

Figure 4-1. Simplistic system architecture expressed in three dimensions

The hosts report their average CPU utilization at one minute intervals. Front-end machines take HTTP requests from the users and dispatch the logic to middleware, which in turn engages the back end to do some heavy lifting. When the process is finished, the middle layer fetches the result from the back end and passes it on to the front end to be served back to a user.

All three groups contain a different number of hosts, according to the frequency and intensity with which they carry out their tasks. Each host sends CPU measurements marked with the hostname of origin and the group the host belongs to.

Managing Large Alerting Configurations

A distributed system is typically composed of hundreds if not thousands of logical components performing some type of work. Present-day systems scale with demand, so some parts might be more volatile than others. In addition, enterprise-level alerting systems are extremely feature-rich, so learning to operate them effectively takes a bit of experience and some attention. The former comes with time (which in itself is a scarce resource), and the latter is split among many other aspects of work. In addition, rich features often give the operators enough rope to hang themselves. This poses an important question: how to maintain desired coverage without burdening operators with the nontrivial, yet mundane and unreliable process of manual updates? Let me break down the problem of alerting at scale into smaller components expressed in terms of monitoring.

Coverage

> Relying on human operators for setting up complex alerting configurations through makeshift scripts is inherently unsound. The system may be composed of moving parts. Unless the operator remembers to amend the configuration after every change, the coverage will deteriorate. This reduces the reliability of detecting alarms.

Detectability

> Coming up with threshold values is not a trivial task. The process is often counterintuitive, and it's simply not feasible to carry out an in-depth analysis for a threshold calculation on every monitored timeseries. A data-driven approach to setting up alarms significantly improves precision.

Consistency

> The value of consistency seems a little abstract, but it is very real. A consistent convention for the structure of alarms drives simplicity and allows for predictability. It can serve as a common interface to read-only information about the current system's state. Chapter 5 explains how to realize this potential through system automation.

Maintenance

> The creation of thousands of alarms and monitors is a labor-intensive task. When a system is cloned to another availability zone, or some parts of it are copied or expanded, a significant amount of work has to be put in reproducing its alerting

configuration. The same goes for tearing down alarms: cruft (irrelevant or outdated code) builds up over time. Cruft doesn't always incur direct costs, but it is often a source of unnecessary confusion. Any attempt to do manual clean-ups introduces the likelihood of accidental damage to the functioning configuration.

The answer to complexity lies in the automation of the process in a way that detects changes in system layout and acts on them before a human operator would. Automation makes alarms systematic and greatly simplifies the preservation of reliable coverage, detectability, and consistency. Additionally, it takes away human effort. Using a managed solution saves lots of operations time, but its most important benefit is a systematic approach to making monitoring better. The change is perceivable by everyone on the team and can be reliably measured with the methods described in Chapter 7.

Addressing the Problems

When the system reaches a certain size, work invested in monitoring may become excessively laborious due to the complexity of the system combined with high rates of change. To solve the problem, the following issues must be addressed directly.

Organize alarms and monitors in a namespace

The alarm setup should reflect the logical topography of the system. Giving alarms namespace-like names brings order and allows you to maintain a hierarchical view. Namespacing provides a convenient abstract container and helps you divide and conquer huge amounts of independent monitors and alarms by functional classification. It's a much better idea to give your alarms systematic rather than descriptive names, such as "All throttled requests for the EU website."

Let me explain this with the familiar three-tier system example. Suppose the system provides some data crunching web service and is located in Europe. The three tiers—front end, middleware, and back end—each run on a separate fleet of hosts. Let me call them frontend, app, and db. Now, assume you want to measure CPU utilization and response latencies in each of the tiers. You could build the structure of alarms and give them names according to the following convention:

```
<service name>.<location>.<tier>.<alarm type>.<alarm>[.<monitor>]
```

Figure 4-2 illustrates the breakdown of alarms. For instance, cruncher.eu.frontend.cpu-util.critical would be the name of an alarm for critical CPU utilization levels on the frontend tier in EU's instance of "cruncher." If you wish to expand the system to serve another geographical region, the overall alarm structure and naming convention would remain the same. Only the location identifier in the namespace would change.

This approach is very powerful. Consistently named alarms provide efficient reporting, ease maintenance, and open the door for using monitors as inputs in automation. Let me point out just a few examples:

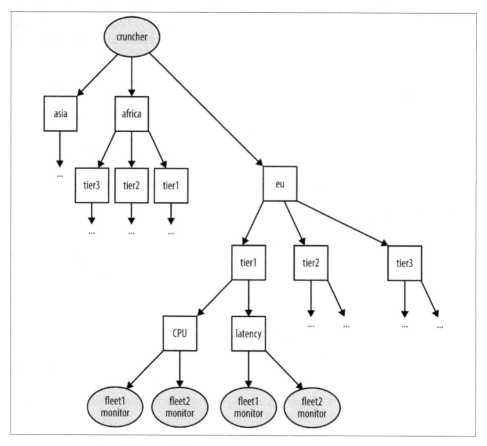

Figure 4-2. Namespaced alarm setup

- Low-level alarms or their aggregates can be used as suppression rules for higher level alarms.
- Transparency into alarms' coverage increases because the alarms may be listed by prefix or regular expression.
- The need to remember alarms by name is replaced by understanding their structure.

Calculate threshold values from metric data

If monitored timeseries are subject to changes in patterns, be it sudden or progressive, their thresholds should be anchored at baselines to reflect the most recent system state. This approach makes detection significantly more accurate.

Imagine that our example system accepts three types of requests for data crunching: small-frequent, medium-regular, and big-infrequent. Let's assume that the *frequency* of submission corresponds to the strain of the front end and that the *size* of requests dictates the load on the back end. The bigger the requests, the less frequently they come in. Suppose you monitor front-end traffic to predict back-end load. In order to do it accurately, you need different thresholds for each type of request, since a few extra big requests have the same effect on load as a huge uptake of small requests.

When the system deals with hundreds of logical entities, each with different load and usage patterns, it's impossible to select a silver-bullet threshold. In such cases, each timeseries is treated as a special case and should get a custom threshold calculated for it.

Where possible, the method of calculation ought to reflect the underlying pattern. For instance, where you want to catch small and relatively infrequent deflections from a steady norm, a threshold based on average of data points and their standard deviation might be most appropriate. For other cases, long streaks of low data points may be discovered by watching for continued occurrences of data points below last week's median or *p40* value. A practical, universal method for many use cases was discussed in more depth in "Data-driven thresholds" (page 67).

Periodically refresh and clean up the configuration

Setting up data-driven thresholds requires their periodic readjustment. Depending on the frequency with which the system gets upgraded, the varying quality of infrastructure, and the system's usage intensity, the metrics will demonstrate changes in patterns at different intervals. The idea is to keep the thresholds coherent with values of the underlying timeseries baseline.

Periodic recalibration also responds to the second type of change, one in the system's internal structure. With time, some parts of the system might go away, while other branches might expand. In the former case, refreshing the alarms is a great opportunity to get rid of cruft, while the latter allows you to extend alerting coverage to the new parts of system.

Suggested Solution

This section attempts to provide a brief specification for creating a small framework that will help you manage thousands of alarms effectively. It combines the previous chapters into a concrete, practical solution, a basic implementation of which should not exceed 400 lines of code in your favorite scripting language.

Think of the solution as a black-box framework composed of two parts: configuration modules and an engine for refreshing the alarms that they describe. The framework is meant to glue together and extend the functionality of your existing monitoring and alerting platform to make maintenance of thousands of alarms a manageable and effortless process.

It breaks the whole configuration down in three hierarchically ordered concepts:

1. *Configuration modules* with specifications of related alarms, organized in period groupings
2. *Alarm specifications* describing alarms as groups of monitors and time evaluations aggregated accordingly
3. *Monitors* pointed at specific timeseries with thresholds calculated according to alarm specification

In its simplest form, the solution can be implemented as a periodically running cron job executing a triple nested "for" loop. The loop iterates over the creation of monitors for each alarm, all alarms for each configuration module, and all modules in a refreshment interval grouping.

The result of the operation is a consistent alarms setup. All alarms and monitors are given namespace-like names, leaving the setup in an ordered, hierarchical structure.

The remainder of this section assumes the ability to programmatically interface with the monitoring and alerting platform, in particular:

- To read timeseries data
- To create and delete alarms and monitors
- To list existing alarms and monitors

Refresh intervals

The task of the engine is to periodically refresh alarms according to their specification. It implements reusable procedures for threshold calculation, alarm setup, and alarm tear-down to provide the following core functionality:

- Interpretation of configuration modules
- Plugging into the monitoring platform to manipulate alarms and monitors according to their specification. This includes their creation, modification, and deletion.
- Calculating thresholds from historical timeseries data with at least one method. An idea for a robust method and simple implementation was presented in Chapter 3.

Alarm refresh intervals are central to the concept of managed alerting. Alarm groups are classified by the frequency with which their monitor configuration is to be reevaluated. I recommend four practical refresh intervals:

Weekly

This is useful for data inputs that change frequently and are critical to the system operation. You should typically set up a relatively small number of alarms against their monitors. A weekly refresh interval is particularly suitable for systems that run on aggressive release schedules, such as continuous integration.

Fortnightly

Similarly to weekly metrics, monitors set up around metrics susceptible to progressive changes in usage patterns should be updated every two weeks, in particular if the changes are caused by uncontrollable external factors, such as traffic levels. If a weekly module defines thousands of alarms to readjust, it makes sense to also place it in the fortnightly grouping.

Monthly

This interval is suitable for metrics reflecting the sustained growth of relatively abundant resources, such as the levels of storage consumed by the customer.

Static

A certain group of monitors does not need periodic adjustments because static thresholds reliably describe them. These alarms are still subject to automatic setup and tear-down, but only once—at software roll-out time. Monitors with static thresholds can be set up for watching utilization limits, loss of availability, or discontinuation of flow. "Static thresholds" (page 66) discusses these examples in more detail.

Figure 4-3 shows how some resources might be classified.

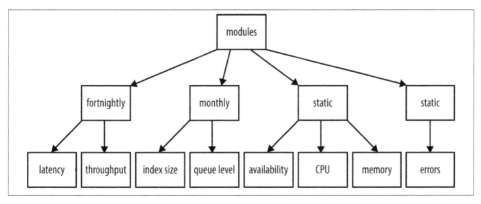

Figure 4-3. Classification of modules for refreshing alarms

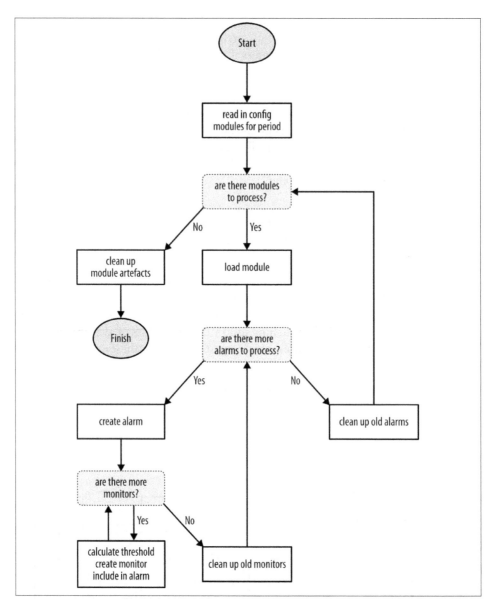

Figure 4-4. The operation of refreshing alarms

Running the engine. The engine gets kicked off periodically from cron. In practice, refresh intervals are groupings of configuration modules. When the engine gets started, it is instructed to process modules belonging to one particular group. All modules from that group are loaded and interpreted, and their configuration is subsequently refreshed. See Figure 4-4 for the process.

The nested loop should carry out three tasks: naming alarms, calculating monitor thresholds, and cleaning up artifacts.

Naming. The engine should construct the namespace name for alarms and monitors as follows:

```
<prefix>.<module>.<alarm>[.<monitor>]
```

where the elements of the name are as follows:

prefix
> An identifier specific to the system. The prefix can be a simple word ("website," "cruncher") or a combination of words describing the system and its properties ("website.eu").

module
> The name of the module containing alarm specifications, ("cpu-util," "network").

alarm
> The name of an alarm aggregate described by each alarm specification.

monitor
> The name of member monitor in the alarm aggregate.

Alarm creation and threshold calculation. For each defined alarm aggregate and its corresponding monitors, the engine should be able to:

- Identify the timeseries for each monitor, extract its recent data points, and calculate a threshold according to specification (see Chapter 3 for a universal threshold calculation method).

- Create the monitor and aggregate it in the parent alarm through one of the aggregation methods (Any, All, or By Count).

- Optionally, outfit the alarm with alerting and ticketing action.

Cleanup procedures. Having read the configuration of the module, the engine should be able to compare the desired configuration state with the current one, created by the previous iterations.

If more monitors are observed after an iteration of each run than are defined in the specification, the excessive monitors can be identified by name and removed. If an alarm specification got removed from the module, this fact should also be detected and the corresponding alarm with all its monitors should be cleaned up.

Writing Modules. Modules are pieces of configuration used in the loop to set up alarms. They list and describe alarm specifications, including the alarm name, its monitors, the type of aggregation, and the alerting configuration. The information extracted from the modules describes the alarms to be created in detail. Such alarm specifications include the following:

1. Alarm name.
2. Monitor names and handles for timeseries on which one or more monitors will be based.
3. Alarm aggregation type ("Any," "All," or "By Count").
4. Threshold calculation tactic. The threshold may be static or adjustable based on recent data point patterns.
5. Alerting information: notification action and ticket definition.

Implementing Modules as Executable Scripts

Configuration modules may be implemented as static data files or dynamic code. I think the second approach is more advantageous if you have the full control over your environment.

A static configuration is hard to write and more voluminous. After you create it, system changes require deployments of new configurations. In contrast, a dynamic configuration specification implemented as a piece of code takes less time and space to write and can figure out any system changes on the go.

The idea is to go with "convention over configuration." Each module describes configuration logic through code instead of static sets of key-value pairs. This way, you avoid hardcoding the system's moving parts, creating a more robust and maintainable configuration. The code will figure out what changed and apply fixes before you would, and there will be no need to edit and peer review configuration files, saving you and your colleagues lots of time.

So implement your configuration as programs that perform intelligence gathering, serialize it, and feed it to the loop.

Very often a single alarm may be supported by a number of monitors. Each monitor relates to the same metric but watches its own dimension. This is why the definition of a timeseries to be monitored should support some basic templating functionality. The following example substitutes the '$(MONITOR)' placeholder in the timeseries template with the respective monitor name. This way, having defined the metric and timeseries just once, you can create a number of related monitors, differing only by the one dimension in the $(MONITOR) placeholder.

Consider the following content returned from a configuration module called "workload":

```
{
    'utilization': {
        'timeseries': {
            'metric': 'cpu-util',
            'dimensions': {
                'tier': 'backend',
            },
            'summary stat': 'avg',
        },
        'monitors': ['critical'],
        'aggregation': 'ALL', # Not really needed for a single monitor.
        'threshold': {
            'trigger': 'above',
            'datapoints': 4, # Alarm after 4 data points
            'static': 0.80, # Trigger when the level raises above 80%
        },
        'ticket': {
            'title': 'Critical levels of CPU utilization.',
            'description': 'Backend fleet CPU util exceeded 80%',
            'impact': 2, # Real threat of possible performance degradation.
        },
    },
    'traffic': {
        'timeseries': {
            'metric': 'requests',
            'dimensions': {
                'request_type': '$(MONITOR)',
            },
            'summary stat': 'n',
        },
        'monitors': ['small-frequent', 'medium-regular', 'big-infrequent'],
        'aggregation': 'ANY', # Trigger if any of the monitors go into alert
        'threshold': {
            'trigger': 'above',
            'datapoints': 5,  # Alarm after 5 data points of unusually
            'percentile': 98, # high traffic levels. Do not let the threshold
            'lower': 50,      # fall below 50 data requests per data point and
            'upper': 1000     # don't let it raise beyond 1000 requests.
        },
        'ticket': {
            'title': 'Unusually high traffic levels for last 5 data points.',
            'description': 'One or more request types come at increased rates.',
```

```
                'impact': 3, # Real threat of possible performance degradation.
            },
        },
    }
```

The configuration describes two alarm specifications.

The first alarm is called "utilization" and contains a single monitor. The monitor watches fleet-wide CPU utilization of the back end and goes into alert state if the threshold of 80% is exceeded for 4 data points. When that happens, the alarm is instructed to file a ticket of relatively high priority.

The second alarm is called "traffic" and includes three monitors observing the number of requests per data point. Because the three types of requests have different usage patterns, threshold values for their monitors are allocated dynamically, based on the 98th percentile in the distribution of historical data points. It was established that a threshold value of below 50 should never be considered a threat, and at the same time, the value should never drift beyond 1000 for any of the monitors. If any of the monitors goes into alert state, a normal priority ticket is filed.

The process executing the loop glues together elements of the namespace to come up with a full name for every monitor and alarm that it creates. It puts together the system name (prefix) with names for module, alarm, and monitor, delimiting them with dots. That way, the CPU alarm handle becomes "cruncher.workload.utilization.critical" and the traffic monitor of the small and frequent type of requests is alarmed on via "cruncher.workload.traffic.small-frequent."

Suppression. The value and applicability of suppressions was explained in "Suppression" (page 57). Manually suppressing large alerting configurations for hundreds of alarms is a mundane and inconvenient task. Seeing alarms as Boolean functions, it is really simple to implement suppression functionality by appending to the aggregate the AND NOT condition pointed at a suppressing condition. That way, through changing a state of a single alarm, alerting for an entire component could be put on hold and an alert storm could be avoided.

Consider the following configuration for the data pipeline discussed in "Case Study: A Data Pipeline" (page 60).

Example 4-1. Simple alerting configuration returned from the "pipeline" module

```
{
    'throughput': {
        'timeseries': {
            'metric': 'processed_items',
            'dimensions': {
                'component': '$(MONITOR)',
            },
```

```
        'summary stat': 'sum',
    },
    'monitors': ['loader', 'processor', 'collector'],
    'aggregation': 'ANY',
    'threshold': {
        'trigger': 'below',
        'datapoints': 1, # Alarm as soon as the pipeline stops
        'static': 1, # Trigger when no items are processed
    },
    'ticket': {
        'title': 'Data pipeline has stopped.',
        'description': 'Unexpected pipeline stoppage.',
        'impact': 2,
    },
    'suppression': 'cruncher.suppressions.pipeline.maintenance'
    }
}
```

The resulting configuration is a single alarm, *cruncher.pipeline.throughput*, consisting of three monitors aggregated in ANY mode. The alarm goes into alert if any single monitor triggers. The threshold condition is set as static and goes off when the number of processed items in the data point is less than one, i.e., when it is equal to zero. This is desired except when scheduled maintenance is to be carried out, during time which the pipeline stops for a short time under full control and supervision.

The final 'suppression' keyword could be interpreted by the engine as attenuating circumstances in which the alarm should not be set off after all. The logical Boolean resulting from the configuration could be expressed as follows:

(cruncher.pipeline.throughput.loader OR cruncher.pipeline.throughput.processor OR cruncher.pipeline.throughput.processor) AND NOT cruncher.suppressions.pipeline.maintenance

See Figure 3-3 for a visual representation. In other words, trigger if any of the monitors is set off unless a suppressing alarm exists and is in alert state.

> To make the suppression process fully hands-off, you should extend the pipeline shutdown procedure programmatically to put the *cruncher.suppressions.pipeline.maintenance* alarm in alert state for the expected duration of the outage, e.g. 1 hour. This way, the operator's only worry is to carry out maintenance and not to deal with instrumentation, which further shortens the expected downtime.

Okay, let's kick the requirements up a notch. Let's say you want to create a more sophisticated configuration, with a separate alert for each component as illustrated in

Figure 3-4. Additionally, you want the monitors to be more intelligent so they can also detect exceptionally low levels of throughput, as opposed to just an absolute discontinuation of flow. Suppose you don't want the pipeline to go any slower than the slowest 5% of performance for a duration of three data points. Still, you want to use common sense limits for both thresholds: the lower at 1 and the upper at 100. This means that if the lowest 5% of historical performance turns out to be 0 items per data point, disregard it and use 1 instead. If, on the other hand, the slowest 5% of data points point to a performance of 100 items per data point interval, stick to the maximum threshold value of 100. Example 4-2 describes this configuration, using the analogy of Example 4-1.

Example 4-2. Granular alarms with calculation of throughput threshold for each component

```
{'loader': {'monitors': ['throughput'],
            'suppression': 'cruncher.suppressions.pipeline.maintenance',
            'threshold': {'datapoints': 3,
                          'lower': 1,
                          'percentile': 5,
                          'trigger': 'below',
                          'upper': '100'},
            'ticket': {'description': 'loader is unexpectedly slow.',
                       'destination': 'teamloader',
                       'impact': 2,
                       'title': 'loader has stopped.'},
            'timeseries': {'dimensions': {'component': 'loader'},
                           'metric': 'processed_items',
                           'summary stat': 'sum'}},
 'processor': {'monitors': ['throughput'],
               'suppression': 'cruncher.suppressions.pipeline.maintenance ' + \
                              'OR cruncher.pipeline.loader.throughput',
               'threshold': {'datapoints': 3,
                             'lower': 1,
                             'percentile': 5,
                             'trigger': 'below',
                             'upper': '100'},
               'ticket': {'description': 'processor is unexpectedly slow.',
                          'destination': 'teamprocessor',
                          'impact': 2,
                          'title': 'processor has stopped.'},
               'timeseries': {'dimensions': {'component': 'processor'},
                              'metric': 'processed_items',
                              'summary stat': 'sum'}},
 'collector': {'monitors': ['throughput'],
               'suppression': 'cruncher.suppressions.pipeline.maintenance ' + \
                              'OR cruncher.pipeline.processor.throughput',
               'threshold': {'datapoints': 3,
                             'lower': 1,
                             'percentile': 5,
                             'trigger': 'below',
                             'upper': '100'},
               'ticket': {'description': 'collector is unexpectedly slow.',
```

```
                    'destination': 'teamcollector',
                    'impact': 2,
                    'title': 'collector has stopped.'},
        'timeseries': {'dimensions': {'component': 'collector'},
                       'metric': 'processed_items',
                       'summary stat': 'sum'}}}
```

All is well, but at three components the configuration starts getting lengthy. If the pipeline was extended by another two components, maintaining this configuration would become a real maintenance burden. This is precisely why static configuration files should be replaced by executable configuration modules, which are easier to maintain and can figure out system settings on the fly. See Example 4-3. The imported `get_com` `ponents` function is assumed to be a part of a system's programmatic interface that can read the list of components at the time when configuration is compiled.

Example 4-3. Module generating alerting configuration

```
from system.pipeline import get_components
# get_components() returns a tuple with component names.
# The following code is assumed:
# def get_components():
#     return ('loader', 'processor', 'collector')

alarms = {}
components = get_components()

for i in range(len(components)):
    alarms[components[i]] = {'monitors': ['throughput'],
        'suppression': 'cruncher.suppressions.pipeline.maintenance',
        'threshold': {'datapoints': 3,
                      'lower': 1,
                      'percentile': 5,
                      'trigger': 'below',
                      'upper': '100'},
        'ticket': {'description': components[i] + ' is unexpectedly slow.',
                   'destination': 'team ' + components[i],
                   'impact': 2,
                   'title': components[i] + ' has stopped.'},
        'timeseries': {'dimensions': {'component': components[i]},
                       'metric': 'processed_items',
                       'summary stat': 'sum'}}
    if i:
        alarms[components[i]]['suppression'] += \
            ' OR cruncher.pipeline.%s.throughput' % components[i-1]
print alarms
```

That's much shorter! Additionally, when the pipeline is extended by the fourth component, the generated configuration will take this fact into account and automatically create an alerting configuration for it, too. This way, there is no need for dispatching update tasks to an operator, no one has to review it for correctness, and there is no obligation to schedule tasks to push out production changes—the alerting configuration should get regenerated the next time the loop runs to refresh alarms.

Extra Features. On top of core functionality, the engine may optionally also implement the following:

- Distributed execution. The periodic update of thousands of monitors supporting hundreds of alarms may necessitate staggered update of alarms from multiple hosts for added reliability and to distribute load on internal monitoring tools.
- The ability to calculate a threshold value for one timeseries, based on data points from a related timeseries. Sometimes the threshold value for one timeseries monitor might be calculated most reliably from data points of a related timeseries. Thus, if you want to alarm when errors exceed 1% of overall traffic, you're setting up the error series' threshold based on a calculation of healthy traffic.
- Suggesting the severities and threshold levels for tickets based on human feedback from the ticketing system (supervised learning).

and much more!

Result

The result of applying the proposed solution is a hierarchically ordered structure of highly effective alarms with increased sensitivity and specificity. Let me provide some anecdotal evidence.

One of the operations teams I worked for introduced this form of managed alerting by implementing a simple engine and slowly migrating a portion of alarms. Figure 4-5 is a rough illustration of the progress as it was taking place during the switch-over. The yellow streak signifies human-created tickets. The green area at the bottom right is the relative amount of tickets created with the managed solution and the gray area at the top represents automated tickets created by legacy settings. Finally, the blue-dotted line reveals in percentage terms the number of alarms migrated to the managed solution. In the end, 85% of migrated alarms produce only 54% of overall tickets. Even with human created tickets taken away, we achieved a noise reduction of more than 23%. Also, notice how the streak of manually created tickets keeps decreasing during the transition—a clear indicative of improved recall.

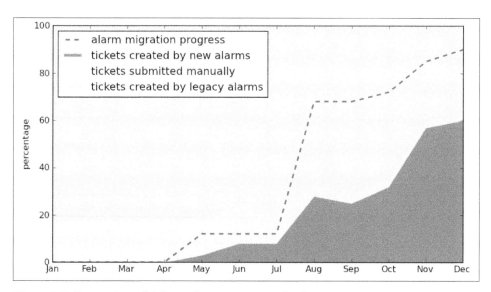

Figure 4-5. Proportion of tickets relative to managed solution coverage

## CHAPTER 5

Monitoring in System Automation

System metrics are a source of valuable information about a system's state. Alarms and monitors evaluating to a Boolean value indicate the current state and operational context of your systems. Thus, you can take advantage of them to programmatically drive resilience and recoverability, while reducing the complexity of human interaction.

Self-Regulating Systems and Autonomic Computing

The holistic approach to the development of self-managing and self-regulating systems is termed *Autonomic Computing* (AC).

By design, an AC system does not require an operator's attention. Instead, it implements a manager application in charge of configuration, governance, protection, optimization, and maintenance of components. The manager is meant to operate in a closed loop of four continuous steps: *monitor, analyze, plan, execute*. The loop opens with monitoring, reading in the information from active sensors. Gathered data serves as a base for analysis, from which the relevant action plan originates. Finally, the stabilizing action is executed and the loop starts over. That keeps the system sustainable.

The autonomic manager requires a good deal of built-in knowledge to work: the system must know what to look for, what decisions to draw from the observations, what alternatives exist for taking an action, and how to execute it. While AC is a broad subject, way beyond the scope of this book, it is well worth mentioning here, as monitoring and alerting are one of the main ingredients in manager's knowledge, at the very least in the plan and analyze steps.

AC's ability to decrease the ratio of operators to managed machines suggests that AC will appear increasingly in the design and development of information systems. This way, the role of monitoring and alerting will be more pronounced than today's eyes and ears of a system—they will become an integrated control loop, pretty much like the autonomic nervous system in a human body.

> For more information on AC specifically, I'd like to refer you to the book *Autonomic Computing* by Richard Murch (IBM Press). This chapter describes how to add a pinch of self-governance to your current systems through the use of monitoring data.

Choosing Appropriate Maintenance Times Automatically

Large-scale systems require regular maintenance operations, such as preventative checks and content updates. These take place during normal system operation and involve removing selected servers from operation. As a result, the system runs at reduced capacity relative to its normal levels and can handle a proportionately smaller load.

Every type of maintenance carries with itself a risk of an outage. However negligible the hazards, they remain real. A minute of downtime at a peak is a lot more costly than the equivalent duration during a trough, and for that reason all maintenance work should be attempted under smallest possible load.

In systems with regular cyclic patterns, peaks and troughs can be clearly distinguished by viewing incoming traffic plots (Figure 5-1). Both extremes of system activity can be assigned to specific hours of the day. It is possible to create an alarm based on the time of day evaluation that goes into alert state during peak. The maintenance processes can be instructed to first consult the alarm state before kicking off their work and to postpone execution when the alert is on. When the demand reaches trough again, the alarm transitions back to a clean state and the processes are given a green light to carry on.

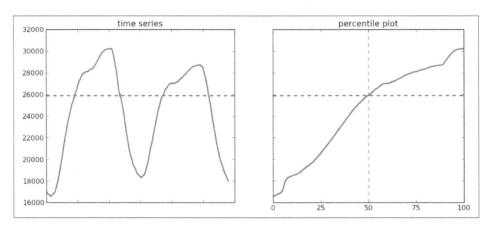

Figure 5-1. Timeseries with two days worth of traffic data points and a corresponding percentile plot of their values

When usage varies in an irregular manner, is unstable, or goes progressively in one direction, the time evaluation rule in the alarm may be replaced by a traffic monitor with a dynamically adjusted threshold, as described by "Data-driven thresholds" (page 67). Such a threshold could be calculated as the *p50* of last week's data points with an additional upper limit set as an appropriate safety value, to avoid capacity reduction when the demand evolves unexpectedly. See Figure 5-1.

In cloud-based settings, this technique can help with autoscaling, or dynamic capacity allocation.

Controlling the Rate of Upgrade

In the same spirit of carrying out work only as resource levels permit, a case could be made for controlling the rate of a staggered system upgrade with the CPU utilization metric.

Suppose you're dealing with a fleet of servers that is to be upgraded. For the upgrade to complete, every server in the fleet must be taken momentarily out of service. Each such operation immediately puts proportionately more load on the remainder of the fleet. It is assumed that once the server gets upgraded it returns to the fleet on its own, and takes on its due proportion of the load. The task is to complete the upgrade in a reasonable time, but without noticeable performance degradation. The main goal is to avoid excessive load put on too few machines.

It has been established that there will be no noticeable performance degradation as long as the CPU util does not exceed 50% on minutely average. The level of utilization during trough varies, but oscillates at around 30%.

The rate of migration may be controlled with a very simple algorithm as depicted the flowchart in Figure 5-2. The loop continuously checks whether more hosts to be upgraded exist in the fleet. If so, fleet-wide CPU utilization is consulted. If the CPU levels remain within the expected threshold, the fleet can be put under a little more strain by taking another host out for upgrade. Otherwise, the process checks back after some time. The hosts are assumed to automatically rejoin the fleet once they're done upgrading.

Because CPU util is such a universal system load indicator, this very simple algorithm accounts for a number of scenarios:

- The upgrade completes in optimal time keeping within the agreed threshold.
- At peak time, when utilization levels rise above 50%, the upgrade process is put on hold to be resumed later when the demand reaches the trough period once again. The process is illustrated in Figure 5-3, showing CPU utilization elevated during before and after the daily peak, relative to baseline levels.

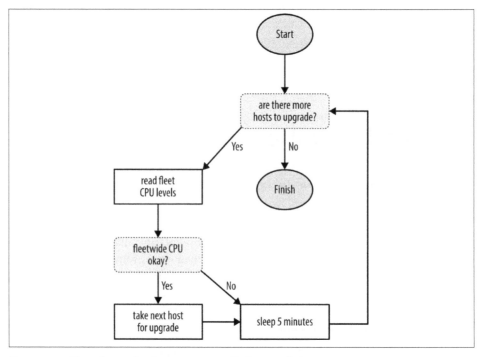

Figure 5-2. Flowchart of utilization-controlled upgrade loop

- If for some reason the upgraded hosts do get back in service as predicted, the upgrade stops at the agreed CPU level and the operator has more time to remedy the situation.
- If during trough the load unexpectedly increases, the CPU util metric will reflect that and the migration will be paused to meet the demand.

Recovery-Oriented Admission Control

Let me bring up one more time a data pipeline example from Chapter 3. Consider a pipeline with three components serially processing a stream of inputs—Loader, Processor, and Collector. For simplicity, I'll refer to them as A, B, and C. The inputs are submitted by multiple independent sources to component A, which enqueues them for processing in B. Component C fetches inputs from B and processes them at an almost constant rate.

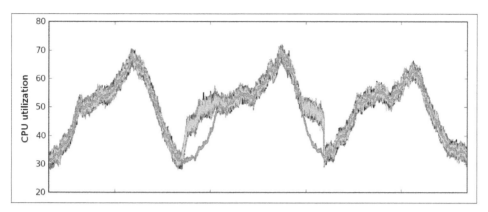

Figure 5-3. CPU utilization during controlled update, plotted against normal levels

The inputs are processed by C in the order of arrival as retrieved from B's FIFO queue. The queue serves as an input buffer handling brief input spikes that cannot be handled immediately by C. Whenever the input arrival rate is higher than the departure rate, the queue builds up a backlog. When the arrival rate decreases, the backlog is steadily drained by C.

The three components record their own monitoring metrics with performance information:

- Component A records the number of incoming inputs as a flow metric and a percentage of admitted inputs as an availability metric.
- Component B records the queue size at any given time—a stock metric with number of elements currently in the buffer.
- Component C records the rate of processing as a throughput metric—its average input processing speed expressed in inputs per minute.

The pipeline operates with limited resources to be cost effective, yet there is no limit on how much load can be submitted by each source at any one time. Data pipelines with unpredictable input burstiness should be considered "best effort" and their operational-level agreements must be defined to reflect that. For that reason, an accompanying SLA defines the maximum allowable end-to-end latency to be one hour, but under normal operation a typical turnaround time should not exceed 15 minutes. It also makes clear that it's better not to admit an input for processing at all than have it breach the SLA latency level.

Suppose the arrival rate has been higher than the departure rate for long enough to accumulate a serious backlog, the clearing of which takes exactly one hour (Figure 5-4). From here on, it makes no sense to admit inputs to the pipeline any faster than the current departure rate, as they will inevitably breach the SLA.

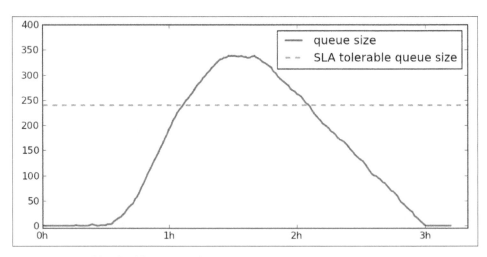

Figure 5-4. Backlog building up in the queue

Knowing the speed of processing (departure rate) and maximum latency as defined in the SLA, you can easily calculate the maximum allowable queue size:

max queue size = SLA defined latency * maximum departure rate

Processing rate is recorded by component C. Let's assume it's at three items per minute. If the SLA-defined latency is 60 minutes and the C component is capable of processing up to 3 items / min, then the queue may reach up to 180 items before the system fails to meet the SLA.

This way, the throughput metric describing the processing rate from component C can be used to set an admission restriction on component A by calculating the threshold of the queue size in component B.

Fine, but suppose the arrival rate stabilizes at around the maximum allowable queue levels. If arrival rate is equal to departure rate all inputs will meet the SLA just barely, but their end-to-end processing latency will still be very poor. This is not always desirable. If the backlog level is steady for days without any improvement then every client will have a uniformly bad experience. At least two problems exist in this solution:

- The clients experiencing poor performance were not necessarily responsible for the build-up, yet they suffer the consequences.
- The buffer does not serve its original purpose anymore: it's unable to capture and deal with occasional, unsustained input bursts as it's clogged with the backlog and drops all inputs above the maximum queue size.

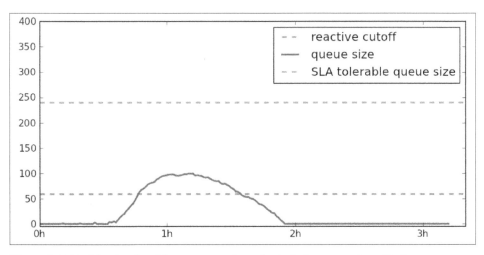

Figure 5-5. Backlog levels with recovery oriented admission control enabled

A further tweaked admission control mechanism could aim at faster recovery to sustainable levels and could look like Figure 5-5.

Suppose that 25% of queue saturation, relative to maximum queue size, would cause an end-to-end latency not exceeding 15 minutes.

Component A accepts all inputs until the queue in component B reaches approximately 25% of the SLA-defined maximum level. At that point component A attempts to drop a percentage of inputs (reflecting relative maximum queue size) for as long as the queue exceeds the limit and not less than the next 4 data points. If the intensity of arrival increases, so does the queue size and so does the percentage of dropped inputs.

This way,

- queue saturation is kept below 25%, enforcing a tolerable latency instead of the maximum allowable one hour when the demand exceeds supply
- when the sustained uptake in inputs is caused by one or a small group of offending sources, they pay the biggest price in terms of number of dropped items
- when the speed of processing by component C changes, max queue size changes its size but the SLA-defined values of one hour and fifteen minutes remain the same

Automated Deployment and Rollback

Traditionally, new software rollouts have required constant attention to ensure timely rollback in case things go awry. However, in agile environments that adopt a continuous integration model or in ones with an aggressive deployment schedule, attempting every single rollout with the low possibility of failure by a human operator becomes too costly. The solution is to push out all recent builds automatically. But what if a small, incremental change introduces a critical fault, capable of bringing down the entire system?

To the rescue comes monitoring-enhanced automated rollback.

The rollout is divided into two phases that are carried out consecutively. First, a fraction of hosts is separated from the total and used for initial sample deployment of the new software version. The metrics on the remainder of the fleet serve as a baseline for comparison. Performance and availability are measured on both groups of hosts, typically by comparing response times and error rates as well as key user metrics. If performance levels on freshly deployed hosts do not reveal any worrisome signs, a staggered deployment to the remainder of the fleet follows. Otherwise, an automated rollback is initiated to minimize any possible negative impact, the deployment pipeline stops, and the issue is brought to the operator's attention. The verification may be repeated during the full rollout and after its completion. If the outcome of the deployment is critical, the system immediately reverts to the latest stable version.

The process is modeled on a finite state machine shown in Figure 5-6. In the illustration, the metrics are consulted twice: first after sample rollout and then after completion of all hosts.

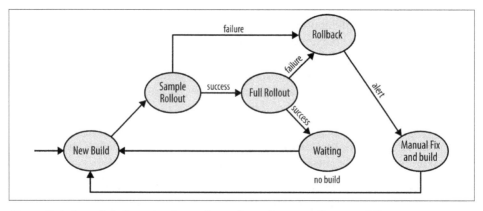

Figure 5-6. A model of monitoring-enhanced continuous rollout workflow

While the idea behind the process is a simple one, its practical implementation has a couple of caveats:

- The performance comparison must take into account the existence of warm-up effects on the servers getting back into service, and disregard them.

- On occasions, false rollbacks may result from unrelated production issues which trick the process into thinking that deployment was at fault.

- Sometimes minimal levels of degradation not impacting the users at all may be the reason for pipeline stoppage.

These are all special cases of false positives. Their existence is typically realized early in the process and dealt with accordingly by threshold tuning.

This enhancement of the process connects the best of both worlds: it does not necessitate the operators to be present at all times during numerous software rollouts, while at the same time it keeps any possible negative impact to an absolute minimum.

The Work Environment

Humans follow incentives, get easily distracted, and are forgetful. Systems keep evolving. Remember this whenever a human operator is expected to become an integral part of an operational process. Some fundamental problems related to monitoring and alerting are due to making false assumptions about human nature; others are due to putting insufficient weight on the importance of change. In general, the problem stems from the perception of how things ought to be, rather than how they actually are. The system is dynamic, many parts are movable, and it's only predictable to a certain degree. The people who designed it are most often not the ones in charge of 24/7 operations. For that reason, the work environment should foster a flexible culture, one that assists in the progress of adaptability and encourages growth.

Keeping an Audit Trail

Responding to alerts means dealing with uncertainty. Even in mature IT organizations outages resulting from changes made by operators, such as new software rollouts, configuration updates, and infrastructure upgrades account for more than 50% of all outages. Keeping an audit trail and consulting it during early outage indications can, therefore, reduce the initial uncertainty in every second case, giving the troubleshooter a massive advantage.

An accurate and complete audit trail does not necessarily have to come at a cost of high manual overhead. It can be greatly automated with the help of a publish-subscribe style messaging system, with elements of the infrastructure automatically publishing updates for routine tasks, such as deployments and upgrades. If the idea isn't clear, think of GitHub's activity feeds. Such a model works best for big organizations running their systems in Service Oriented Architecture (SOA). Any single team in charge of service could subscribe to an audit trail feed of upstream services, so that any upstream changes are easily identifiable on a timeline.

Working with Tickets

Most operation teams at any given time designate an on-duty operator (*the On-call*) whose job it is to respond to incoming alerts and manage the ticket queue. The theory states that on a typical day the On-call comes in to work, opens the ticket queue, and iterates through the list of tickets in descending order of severity. However, the work is prone to interruptions. When a new issue of high enough severity arrives in the queue, the On-call is expected to drop whatever he is working on to deal with the incoming event.

This theory doesn't always apply in practice. More typically, the On-call comes in, opens the queue with a list of all-too-familiar, inactionable tickets and glances over to catch any new arrivals. When the queue grows big enough, new arriving medium-severity tickets are not even noticed in the crowd of predecessors and therefore the time of the initial response goes up.

On occasion the managers notice an unmanageable amount of tickets in the queue and typically try to deal with the problem by allocating more resources. Here are the three most common ways in which this is done:

Incentive Schemes
> Letting engineers know that the count of tickets they resolve is a measure of their performance

Allocating a Secondary On-Call
> Getting another pair of hands to work on tickets

Occasional Queue Cleanups
> Getting an entire team to clean the queue periodically for a day

All of these methods are equally ineffective because they all rely on the same flawed assumption: that a ticket generated from an alert is a unit of work rather than an indication of a problem in the system. In reality, the root of the problem is the impaired detectability. To solve it, the alerting configuration should be made more effective.

Anomalous events that pose no customer impact should be recorded but they must not be a reason for waking up operators in the middle of the night only to confirm the system's sanity. All alarms that trigger on nonissues should be done away with if there is no evidence that the resulting alerts are actionable. If this policy is not followed, false alarms will cause more harm than good. There are only two ways in which one can respond to nonissue: ignore it or overreact.

In the former case the detrimental effects will be prolonged and difficult to measure. Initially, the notifications will introduce a mild level of noise; the ticket queue will grow but it will be difficult to pinpoint the reason for this. After a while the operators will get desensitized to real problems and will stop taking tickets seriously. This is where the ball gets dropped. If the neglected problem develops into an outage, no one will understand why the operator had ignored it in the first place.

In the latter case, overreaction, the outcomes can be quite immediate. Let me illustrate this with an example of alarming on cache evictions in a memcache fleet. A cache eviction is dropping a relatively old entry from the cache in view of a memory shortage to make some space for more frequent entries. Cache evictions are not by themselves an indicative of a problem or degraded performance. Let's assume that a high-priority ticket is created when cache evictions are detected. An ambitious operator might at first try to look for the root cause, but failing to find anything obvious he decides to at least put the alarm out of alert state by restarting the memcache fleet. Now the cache is empty and needs to regenerate itself. In the process the web server fleet must work much harder because it is not being relieved by the caching layer, introducing strain and putting the system at unnecessary risk.

Root Cause Analysis

The term root cause tends to be interpreted differently by everyone, which leads to numerous breakdowns in communication. This issue can be clearly identified in the process of assigning a root cause at ticket resolution time. The outcome depends on the point of view of the person resolving the ticket. Let me explain the confusion with this vague example: If an operator aims at rebooting a subset of hosts in sequence but mistakenly manages to reboot the entire fleet at once, is this an operator error, misallocation of responsibilities, lack of fine-grained tools, bad ACLs, or a problem with the process? With each interpretation, the blame is pointed at someone else. In effect, it depends on who gets asked the question. That subjective approach is not very constructive but there are ways to avoid falling into this trap.

Root Cause Analyses (RCA) are carried out to determine the reasons that major events cause detrimental effects on the production environment. The main goal of RCA is to establish the real reason behind the fault in order to take an informed corrective action and prevent future recurrences. Effective RCAs must have two objectives in mind: they must be carried out with sufficient depth and they must not focus on personal assignment of blame. When executed to find the answers rather than a scapegoat, it quickly becomes apparent that the situation was a lot more complex than we initially believed and that the problem could have possibly been prevented at many levels with varying degree of effort.

The Five Whys

A practical RCA can be carried out via the Five Whys method. The method was developed by Sakichi Toyoda, the founder of Toyota Industries Co., and later used extensively at Toyota Motor Corporation as an efficient problem-solving tool and one of the core concepts in the Toyota production system.

The method also finds its application in carrying out analyses of system failures. It provides a practical approach to discovering causal relationships of events at several levels and draws a clear distinction between technical difficulties, the situational circumstances that led to them, and deficiencies in planning and resource allocation.

The method instructs us to ask approximately five consecutive, related "Why?" questions about the event, starting with the symptoms. Table 6-1 illustrates the question chain with a generalized example.

Table 6-1. Generalized Example of a Five Whys Analysis

"Why" Question	Answer
Why were the symptoms observed?	Because of an immediate cause.
Why did the immediate cause occur?	Because of an exceptional condition.
Why did the exceptional condition arise?	Because of a special circumstance.
Why was the special circumstance not handled properly or in time?	Due to insufficient X or excessive Y.
Why was there a lack of X or too much Y?	...

The first two questions focus on immediate technical cause and its source, the third "why" tries to find out more about the circumstances that led to the problem, and the last two questions focus on organizational inefficiencies and misallocations and their origin. It's worth noting that the answers further down in the chain become more subjective and open to interpretation. They serve well as conclusions, but may not necessarily be accurate.

The Five Whys method provides only an abstract skeleton for a causal chain of events. In order to get to the bottom of issues, assumptions and deductive logic will not suffice. A fair share of hands-on log mining and data analysis must take place in the process. Let's consider the analysis on a more concrete example:

A batch processing system does not accept new job submissions. Why not? The inspection of running jobs shows that a backlog was accumulated. Why the backlog? Performance graphs show reduced processing throughput. Why reduced throughput? Long delays are observed while processing certain batches. Why only selected batches? These batches differ in structure and contain attributes not understood by the system. Why does the system not understand them? The batches were built contrary to technical specification.

Asking five whys uncovered two contributing factors: submission of bad input and insufficient input validation. Of the two the root cause is the lack of sufficient input validation—accepting malformed input should never be the reason for an outage. The corrective action involves implementation of an input validation and rejection mechanism.

Extracting Categories. A portion of answers to the questions in the Five Whys analysis may be used to form a list of root cause classifying categories. Highly specific classifiers are not very useful as there are too many of them and they get outdated too fast. On the other hand, a classifier that's too open-ended does not convey meaningful information for the purposes of reporting. Well formulated categories come as a result of generalized answers to the centermost of the five asked questions.

The following list of suspected causes was compiled through Five Why analysis from a sample of tickets. The resulting twelve categories are divided into three main groups: technical errors, monitoring problems used for measuring precision and recall, and other, unidentified faults. The categories describe specific shortcomings; they do not include coinciding events and contributing factors, such as content updates or specific maintenance work that may have led to the problem.

Software Error
> Problems as a direct consequence of software flaws. The category includes software bugs, architectural limitations, and gross inefficiencies leading to perceivable impact to be eliminated through the rollout of patched versions.

Misconfiguration
> Faults originating from suboptimal or incorrect system settings.

Hardware Error
> Physical faults with a visible effect on the system's operation.

Network Error
> Diminished performance traceable to deterioration of the underlying network link.

Data Corruption
> Faults incurred in the process of transmission, storage or extraction of data.

Operator Error
> Faults that arise as a consequence of mishandling the system through the use of operator privileges. Operator errors come from negligence, inexperience, and the lack of a deep understanding of the system. They occur during migrations, host upgrades, and cruft cleanups, typically due to overaggressive deactivation of parts of the system or lack of adequate preparation.

Capacity Limit

Issues resulting from running a system for which workload exceeds capacity in normal operation. This category excludes capacity exhaustion caused by operator errors or critical software bugs leading to saturation of computational resources.

Dependency Error

Faults generated by downstream services on which the system depends. Example dependencies include databases, external workflow engines, and cloud services. When dependencies experience downtime they may impair the dependent system's functionality.

False Alarm

Tickets that come as a result of oversensitive monitoring and bugs in monitoring applications. The incidence of false alarms should be reduced to avoid noise.

Duplicate Ticket

Multiple tickets informing about the same issue that come as a result of insufficient aggregation. Only the first ticket in the group should be considered as a valid alert. The remainder introduces noise and should be discarded as duplicates. Their incidence should be reduced to avoid desensitization in operators.

Insufficient Monitoring

Tickets created manually as a result of deficiencies in monitoring. This category applies when a lack of relevant metrics and alerting configuration allows a preventable problem to go unnoticed and develop into a critical issue.

Unknown/Other

Unidentified or unclassified group of problems. It is often feared that the "Other" category serves as a dumping ground for neglectful investigators and it is often decided to remove the "Other" classifier. This approach increases operator effort and reduces the accuracy of classification. When the number of items classified as "Other" grows out of proportion, it is a sign that the classification process may be flawed.

Dealing with Anomalies

In large-scale system operation failure is a norm. Transient errors often occur very briefly, sometimes in spikes at unpredictable intervals. Low percentage errors occur continuously during normal system operation and constitute a tiny percentage of failed events (not more than 0.1%) in context of the all successful events.

Both types of errors will crop up at large scale and are seen as potential threats to availability levels agreed in the SLAs. This belief is not unjustified, but it is important to keep a healthy sense of proportion as the real threat to availability comes from long lasting outages and not occasional errors. Despite that fact, there is a tendency for more human effort to be invested in root cause analysis of petty issues than prevention of potentially disastrous outages.

Having said that, low percentage errors are by no means unimportant. They do happen for a reason and often are an early indication of hitting resource limits. This is not necessarily a bad thing—it might just mean that your fleet is not overscaled and that you get optimal value for money! As long as the errors stay at negligible levels, there might be other, more urgent things to worry about.

Learning from Outages

When high-visibility, unplanned outages hit the system they should be dealt with accordingly—a quick response followed by root cause investigation. The root cause is used to drive the corrective action, such as implementation of a safety trigger or rearrangement of components to limit performance bottlenecks.

But the failure could be embraced even further. There is a wealth of information in outages since what we imagine the system to be is not necessarily what's really out there. Outages driven by extreme conditions often uncover unexpected behaviors of subsystems and components. Only a fraction of them might be relevant to current issue resolution, but the remainder may be an indication of weak spots where they are least expected. There is a strong case for observing failure beyond the root cause, paying special attention to recoverability and resilience of all subsystems and their components.

Using Checklists

Checklists are an extremely useful device for reducing human error. They strengthen consistency in following procedures and shorten the time otherwise spent on creating improvised solutions. They are particularly suitable for dealing with high severity events. Many of us experience temporary amnesia and panic states in the initial period of getting under pressure. Opening an event response with a checklist is a great way to deal with this.

Well conceived checklists must have a few characteristics:

- They must be used for nontrivial tasks that bear a degree of responsibility.
- They must be designed to check for essentials.
- They must be short.

If the above conditions are not met then some or all of the team will not follow the checklist. This defeats the whole purpose.

Checklists may have a detrimental effect if used inappropriately. Let me name as an example a daily checklist to rule out all faults experienced historically.

Going through a long list of past problems to verify their absence is a boring and frustrating task. It is carried out more reliably by system alarms. A quick peek into the ticket queue combined with a dashboard glance-over should yield the same, if not better, results. If it doesn't, then either the dashboard or the alarm configuration needs to be improved.

 Some things are easier to put into existence than to remove, and checklist items definitely belong to this category. For a checklist to be effective, their items must be meaningful and there must be very few of them.

Creating Dashboards

Dashboards are a collection of top-level performance indicators, all gathered in the same place to serve as a central point of reference. They are great tools for conveying the essentials of state information in real time. Dashboards are created by system administrators soon after they identify a set of higher-order performance metrics. Frequent, proactive examination of these metrics is essential and helps operators and administrators to stay on top of things.

Creating dashboards is the art of communicating a lot with little. Good dashboards start with high-level overview, assisted by succinct explanation, and allow an operator to click through to ever finer levels of detail. They use browser's real estate wisely. Poor dashboards present the viewer with information overload and the data is not organized systematically.

Dashboards are created to give an overview of the system but they are sometimes used for watching in anticipation of a problem. That's fine as long as observing timeseries isn't someone's full time job. Allocating people solely for following data point fluctuations is considered a rewarding job only by very few. Even though our brains are superior pattern matching engines, expecting humans to act as an alerting system is inherently unreliable. It makes more sense to invest the time into creating a sophisticated monitoring system.

Service-Level Agreements

SLAs pose a baselining danger. If a team is facing SLAs that can't be met for purely technical reasons, there are exactly two things that can happen: the team may use unrealistic SLA as the baseline for monitoring or ignore it and use the system's real baseline, calculated on current availability and performance figures. The former solution has a more detrimental effect on meeting the SLA due to the amount of false positives it generates, yet the latter solution is almost never adopted, at least not initially.

Here is why false positives exacerbate the problem: Suppose an alarm was created with the threshold reflecting an SLA that cannot be met. As a result the alarm constantly goes in and out of alert. Suppose this happens a couple of times a day. Being used to frequent alerts, the operators stop investigating the source of the problem and leave the ticket alone (they are "maturing the ticket"). Once the SLA levels are back to normal the operator closes it off. All is well until a real issue is reported and the operator ignores it, as the problem is assumed to be self-recoverable. The service levels deteriorate even further, subjecting users to an even poorer experience. Tickets that are ever-present in the queue will desensitize operators.

 Unrealistic SLAs can be avoided. Inviting a senior member of the technical team to service contract negotiation meetings is always a good idea.

Preventing the Ironies of Automation

With time, increasingly more manual processes become automated. The operators, while still tasked with supervision of the system, will be less and less in touch with system internals. The skill deteriorates when not used. These ironies of automation can be countered, but the process requires conscious cultural effort:

1. Seek simplicity. Complexity breeds confusion and leads to errors. Simplicity goes hand in hand with consistency. Minimizing confusion and having everyone on the same page expedites recovery.

2. Automate. You will save time, reduce costs, improve reliability, and have a lot of fun while doing it.

3. Monitor extensively. Record every relevant piece of information, know where it came from, and be able to pull it up at any time.

4. Keep SOPs short. De-automation of one end defeats the purpose of automation on the other. The longer your SOP, the higher the likelihood of error.

5. Encourage learning. Operators are hired for quick and effective response. Some develop strong intuition, but even intuition must be backed by experience, and frankly, it's not enough. Operators must know what they are doing. It makes sense to give up some productivity in favor of a deepening understanding of the system.

Culture

The human element plays the crucial role in the process. As a result, effective monitoring depends heavily on the right culture of the organization. A strong culture is hard to define in absolute terms but certain characteristics are universal. Successful cultures that drive effectiveness will encourage consistency, trust in technology, and a healthy sense of proportion. Ineffective cultures will do the opposite. In particular

- Assigning a high degree of personal responsibility to boring tasks will sooner or later result in negligence
- Allowing for multi-step manual procedures guarantees that some of the steps will be missed for a portion of the time
- Punishing everyone for one person's mistake with added bureaucracy introduces unnecessary overhead

In all of the above, the problem exists in the process, not in the operator. Processes can be improved by review, streamlining, and automation. Realizing that yet still keeping the human operator in the picture helps to drive a healthy culture: one that nudges even the wrong people to do the right thing and turns problems into solutions instead of blame.

CHAPTER 7
Measuring Success

One can recognize the quality of collaboration by how success is measured. The task of fostering the culture rests mainly with managers. The onus of maintaining a top-notch configuration and event response is on operators. Measuring success, however, is a collaborative effort, one requiring a fair amount of common sense and resisting the urge to positively exaggerate results. Effective alerting configurations are hard to build and even harder to measure. This chapter deals with measuring qualitative changes with quantitative means.

Managers and the employees, here typically systems engineers, work towards common goals but some of their priorities may vary. Engineers like getting things done; managers like when things get done. In other words, engineers focus on problem solving while managers put emphasis on efficiency of execution and reporting. The two priorities are not conflicting as long as a healthy balance is maintained. If it is not the case, reporting can become burdensome.

The problem is real: the more time spent by engineers on accounting, the less of it goes into doing actual work. But it's not just about overhead. When people see no value in accounting (and if you hire smart people, as most IT businesses do, they most likely have valid reasons for it) they might still carry out the tasks you ask but are more likely to do it neglectfully. Ironically, inaccurate accounting makes it harder to reliably identify pain points, which, when resolved, could free up engineers to work on more exciting stuff.

For these reasons measuring quality must not be effortful, otherwise quality assessment will come at a very high cost and with dubious credibility. Fortunately, it is possible to draw reliable conclusions about the nature of issues and the workload required to deal with them from basic classification and a set of timing metrics.

The Feedback Loop

Mature organizations run full-featured monitoring systems with an ability to display metrics and send alerts. Monitoring systems are complemented by issue tracking systems, specialized databases where alerts are stored in the form of tickets (Figure 7-1).

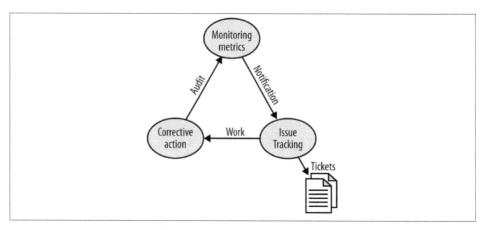

Figure 7-1. The monitoring feedback loop

A ticket contains information about a specific problem and a set of meaningful properties, such as the source of the problem, its severity, time of the notification, time taken to respond and resolve the issue, and finally, the suspected root cause. Accumulated over time, tickets are a great source of feedback about the types of experienced problems, time spent on resolving them, and certain aspects of the quality of work.

In essence, tickets are a rich source of information and a baseline for further improvements. In the remainder of this chapter I will assume that every alert results in a ticket and will use the term ticket and alert interchangeably.

Root Cause Classification

Tickets can be divided into those generated automatically by alarms and those filed manually by humans. All tickets are created for a good reason but only some for a valid reason. All tickets, irrespective of their validity, should have a proximate cause assigned.

Tickets come as a result of faults originating from a set of finite causes. They can, therefore, be binned into groups by their suspected causing factor. The process of classification is simple: at the time of resolution, the operator assigns to the ticket its most appropriate proximate cause from a drop-down menu or via tagging functionality. The suspected cause does not have to be unconditionally correct; it is enough if the suspicion is strongly founded.

The resulting classification serves as a source of wisdom as to what the perceived major pain point is. Reported data can be used for the simplest form of analysis where the output is interpreted in terms of relative proportions.

A Short Story of a Long Classifier List

One of the operations teams I worked for maintained a list of close to one hundred problem category bins. This number was fluctuating with a strong tendency to increase. The list included tens of entries with very specific historical root causes (such as "X of Y failed due to Z"), that were unlikely to ever appear again after upgrades. At one point the categories became so abundant that one ticket could have fit into several categories depending on the interpretation, though only one category was allowed. Consequently, each ticket ended up being assigned to the first matching category found either from the top or from the bottom of the list and rarely from the middle. With time, the "Other —Unknown" category, easily accessible as the last one on the list, gained popularity as it required virtually no cognitive effort to classify a ticket that way. When this fact came to light, we decided to abandon the generic category to prevent its "abuse."

Ironically, despite maintaining the culture of problem classification for each ticket, no one seemed to look at the resulting reports, at least not conclusively.

One particular recurring issue with degraded quality of output, later definitively identified to be a timing problem, had been classified with fifteen separate root cause tags including local data corruption, hardware failure, a software bug, managing system being out of sync, and even database outage.

It seems that in the process of classification we forgot what purpose it was serving: the identification of major pain points and an estimated portion of time spent on fighting them. Instead we were gathering counters for specific failure cases with a level consistency that left a lot to be desired.

I drew two simple lessons from that experience.

1. Human attention is limited and it is practical to keep a list of categories to a reasonable minimum.

   Think of a number of slices you'd like to see on a pie chart. It is impractical to have too many categories. If they get too abundant you will have to account for the unintended negligence of the person responsible for classification, increased error rate, and lack of suitability for later analysis.

2. Generic categories are universal and better suited for reporting.

   There is no point in adding specific failure causes to the category list. They will probably evolve at the same pace as your system and you might not keep up with adding and removing them. In this case, it is perfectly OK to aim for accuracy over granularity: you can break down results to achieve finer granularity at any time, that is, through in-depth introspection of tickets in the offending category. Correcting the accuracy of classification would be a much tougher task.

Timing

Tickets contain timing information in the record of their life time. These are the times of ticket creation, initial response, successive updates, and resolution. Timing information is recorded without conscious effort and when analyzed on a group of tickets, it yields an interesting set of observations about delay and recurrence.

The lifetime of a ticket looks roughly as follows: When the ticket is originally created it takes a certain amount of time to attract resolvers attention. Initial response time typically depends on the severity with which the ticket arrives as dictated by an internal SLA. The ticket then is being worked on by one or more resolvers. The work is typically carried out in multiple steps, and progress is noted through successive updates. Having verified applied fixes, the ticket gets closed off.

Timing information gathered in the process can be used to form conclusions based on a set of observations:

initial response delay (IRD)
    IRD = initial ticket update – ticket creation date

ticket resolution delay
    TRD = resolution time – ticket creation date

time spent resolving (TSR)
    TSR = resolution time – initial ticket update

Additionally, ticket creation timestamps can show the cyclic nature of an issue—for instance, due to regular maintenance—and may be indicative of insufficient capacity, too aggressive update stagger, or oversensitive monitoring, which the following section explains in more detail.

Ticket Reporting

While monitoring helps in detection and dealing with urgent issues, reporting on alerting data focuses on identification of lingering problems which, when untreated, generate huge amounts of unnecessary effort over time. I like to think of them as a tax imposed on the team in form of additional labor. When the operational pain is small enough and distributed equally among team members we all agree to pay it, sometimes forgetting that it builds up to multiple effort-weeks per year. Ticket reporting allows operators to identify the pain points and to invest the time in resolving them.

Frequency of Incidence

The ticket database can be used to report on relative frequency of incidence. The report is based on classification of tickets according to characteristics of the researched fault, such as the symptoms (the ticket's subject), suspected root cause, or severity. The data can be presented in a pie chart that illustrates relative proportions, as depicted on Figure 7-2. The figure illustrates dependency and software errors and reaching capacity as the biggest pain points. This type of visual introspection gives an idea of where the operational effort is spent and facilitates making decisions about resource allocation.

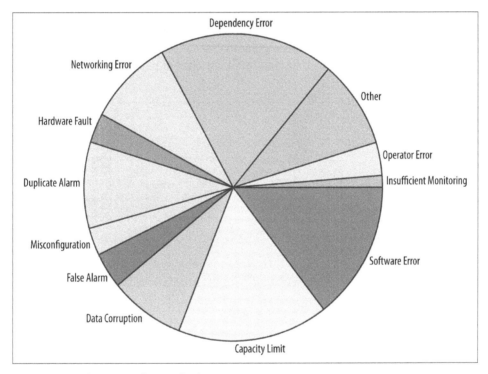

Figure 7-2. Relative incidence of tickets per root cause

Incidence Times

To illustrate the idea with an example, suppose a system is updated daily with a database of users. The update procedure happens twice a day at a 12h interval and takes 0.5h to complete. The maintenance is performed on a fleet of 12 hosts, and involves taking the updated host out of service. Shutting down the entire fleet for a full hour is an unacceptable loss of availability; the team therefore decides to trade off a smaller percentage of reduction in capacity for a larger portion of time during which the staggered upgrade is performed. The questions are: how much can the capacity be reduced, for how long, and at what times of the day to minimize the impact? If the system utilization has peaks and troughs, performing updates during peak guarantees that most users will be affected by it and is therefore costly. Reducing capacity too low puts the system at risk of availability loss. Increasing stagger times extends the duration of maintenance and therefore the system is at risk for a longer period of time. Inadequate selection of these trade-offs leads to an increased number of tickets at specific times of the day. This implies either one of two undesirable things: hitting capacity limits or oversensitive monitoring.

A histogram of the frequency of incoming tickets per hour may reveal patterns of increased alarms. Where increase in ticket incidence overlaps with peak time one is most likely dealing with hitting capacity bottlenecks. Figure 7-3 shows two periods of increased ticket incidence: 8 AM and midnight. High ticket incidence during trough periods might hint at tickets caused by regular maintenance. Interestingly, processes that get kicked off from cronjob tend to manifest themselves at midnight.

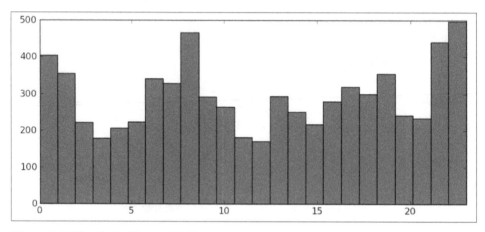

Figure 7-3. Hourly incidence of tickets

Time to Respond and Time to Resolution

It is fair to assume that easy tickets are picked out from the queue first. With that in mind, looking at initial response times (IRD) is likely to reveal areas of knowledge deficiency and the need for more training.

Changes in average time spent resolving a ticket (TSR, measured as the difference in time of initial response and time of resolution) points to ticket groups that are largely inactionable. Tickets that are worked on actively take considerably less time to resolve than those which are put away for "maturing" (when the symptoms are waited out). Figure 7-4 shows the causes of the slowest five groups of tickets and the interquartile mean of their TSR.

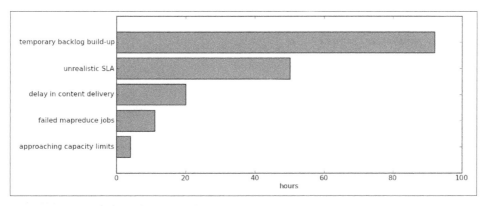

Figure 7-4. Groups of tickets with slowest resolution times

Measuring Detectability

False Positives and False Negatives

A false positive happens when an alarm goes off on a nonissue, an event having no or negligible user impact. A false negative, on the other hand, happens when a legitimate fault does not trigger an alert and goes unnoticed. Effective alerting aims at reducing the incidence of both phenomena.

Conversely, a true positive is a correctly detected alertable event and a true negative refers to no alarm when in fact none was necessary. See Figure 7-5.

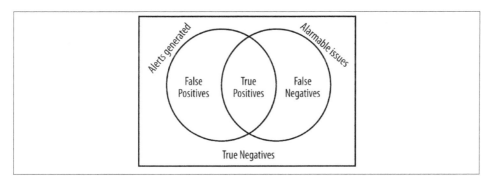

Figure 7-5. Detectability

Therefore, alertable issues are the sum of true positives (tickets created for correctly identified issues) and false negatives (situations in which a ticket has not been generated due to insufficient alarm sensitivity or coverage). The sum of generated tickets, on the other hand, includes true and false positives (Table 7-1).

Table 7-1. Contingency Table of Type I and Type II Errors

	alertable issue	non-issue
alarmed on	true positive	false positive
ignored	false negative	true negative

The implications of false negatives are obvious to everyone: the issues slip under the radar. This is never good, especially when the problem remains undetected for an extended period of time and long enough to be discovered by the users. Finding out about problems from customers is not a place any of us wants to be.

False positives, on the other hand, result from oversensitive threshold values. Some might view the problem only in terms of resource overallocation, thinking that there is no immediate harm in keeping the technical staff just a little busier by responding to events more frequently. But that is incorrect: eventually oversensitivity of alerting leads to desensitization in humans: if 50% of alerts are false alarms, a new event will have less than 50% chance of being taken seriously. If most alerts are false alarms then when the real issue finally comes up it is almost guaranteed to be incorrectly rejected on an assumption that the alarm is false.

False alarms come in two flavors: false positives and monitoring software errors triggered by software bugs and errors in metric collection. In other words, false alarms are a superset of false positives. Reduction monitoring software bugs is outside the scope of this discussion, but it should be mentioned that false alarms resulting from them drive down precision of the decision in the same way as false positives.

Precision and Recall

Precision is a ratio of true positives to the sum of true and false positives. In the current context, it's a ratio of tickets generated for a valid reason to the total of all created tickets.

Calculation of precision relies on the root cause classification discussed in the previous section: the number of true positives can be interpreted as the count of all created tickets less those to which "false alarm" classification has been assigned. To restate that in the form of an equation

precision = (all tickets - false alarm tickets) / all tickets

Recall is the ratio of tickets created for a valid reason to the number of alertable issues.

There exists a problem in an exact definition of "alertable." The exact meaning depends on the policy of the organization—what events are considered impactful. It is hard to precisely estimate the number of alertable issues that slipped under the radar, but their number corresponds to the number of tickets manually created by users. Naturally, it is not a 1:1 relationship, as some user issues may result from lack of understanding rather than system malfunction, but on the other hand not all alertable issues are reported. At any rate, higher recall does correspond to fewer external reports of system malfunction.

recall = (all tickets - false alarm tickets) / (all tickets - false alarm tickets + user tickets)

Both measures are relatively hard to acquire because their calculation relies on human input. In the case of precision, a human operator must identify the incoming ticket as false. Recall relies on the interaction with users or operators and their ability to report undetected problems.

If everyone is on the same page when it comes to handling tickets—great! If not, then the values of precision and recall will carry proportionately less meaning.

The F-Measure

With precision and recall defined, it's time for F-measure—a weighted, harmonic mean of precision and recall. As a score combining the two qualitative factors, the F-measure serves as the universal indicator for effectiveness of alerting configurations. In its most generic form, it is calculated as follows:

F = 2 * (precision * recall) / (precision + recall)

The resulting F score reflects the quality of the current alerting configuration. It is a good idea to track it, along with precision and recall, on a monthly basis and watch all three of them respond to improvements as these get implemented (see Figure 7-6).

Transition to Automated Alarms

If, encouraged by Chapter 4, you decide to switch over to automatic generation of alerting configuration then in addition to evidencing qualitative improvements in monitoring with precision and recall metrics, I recommend juxtaposing the effectiveness of the legacy and the new solution during the switch-over process. Given that the transition process will happen gradually, there are four things that you should keep track of on a weekly or monthly basis:

1. Percentage of alarms migrated to the managed solution
2. Amount of tickets submitted by humans

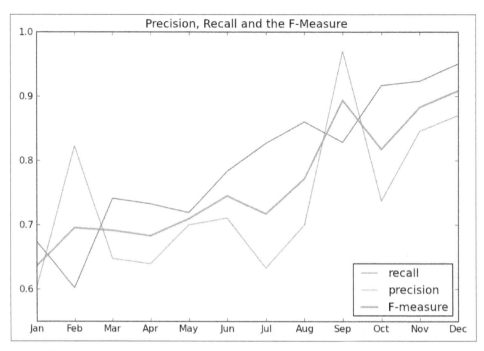

Figure 7-6. Progressive improvement in quality of alerting configuration

3. Amount of tickets generated by legacy alarms

4. Amount of tickets generated by your managed solution

Figure 4-5 shows an example result of such transition.

Maintenance Overhead

Monitoring and alerting are a means and not an end for vast majority of organizations. At the same time they are critical to system operation—monitoring is your eye into the system, and when you wish to look away alerting becomes the ear. As much as we would like for those two pieces of instrumentation to always function and never break, in reality they do require maintenance. Downtime of the monitoring system does not translate directly to downtime that impacts the user, but it does put the rest of the system at risk. It does, therefore, make sense to keep track of yearly failure count and cumulative downtime of the monitoring system.

The work with monitoring should boil down to altering the configuration metadata to reflect the desired state, and no further manual work (writing custom scripts to setup or clean up alarms) should be necessary. If it is, then the number of engineer-hours spent on dealing with setting up alarms manually might add up to weeks per year. Automation through managed alerting configurations solves this problem; it might be a good idea to invest the time in implementing it to avoid paying this unnecessary tax.

How (Not) to Measure

It is too easy to use trivial indicators like number of alerts received, tickets resolved, alarms, or metrics existing in the system. While these numbers might convey some information, mostly about scale, they do not tell the story and are not very useful without context. As tempting as it seems to measure accuracy of alerting by the number of alerts generated, it's not the way to do it—the F-measure is a more reliable score.

The really interesting questions have a qualitative nature and are more difficult to track:

- What is the quality of our work (e.g., with tickets)?
- Do we learn in the process?
- How many alerts were actually necessary? Have we missed many issues? How many? How serious?
- What is the total cost of ownership (TCO) for maintaining the current monitoring configuration? What is their penetration rate of metrics? Do we look at and make use of our data?

Coming up with meaningful answers involves interpretation of numbers, not just their mere presentation. The following questions might point you in the right direction:

- Context—How have we been doing historically? Are we doing better or worse than others? Where are we heading?
- Validity—Is there a way to verify findings? Are the drawn conclusions relevant?
- Reproducibility—Can the findings be reproduced? Can I rerun the procedure next week or month for comparison?

CHAPTER 8

The Principles

I would like to close this book with a few principles that I consider fundamental for effective work with monitoring and alerting. I put them at the end as a summary of the message I'm trying to send. If I were to boil these principles down to a just a few sentences, they would read as follows.

Get in the Habit of Measuring

Monitoring is about detecting state changes from fluctuating timeseries or, more generally, about extracting meaning from the data in real time. The first step on the way to systematic discovery of useful information is to make a habit of measuring relevant information.

Collect the data starting with important metrics. Focus on top-level performance indicators and keep adding related ones as necessary. Try to understand the relationships between subsystems and their components. Do strong relationships exist? Are they invariant? Are they of linear or exponential nature? Do they have a confounding factor?

Secondly, it is very important to *look at* the gathered data. Too often the measurements are never analyzed. It's okay not to look at all the generated metrics—you want these to be there for you just in case. If, however, data collection involves human effort then not looking at the outcome renders data collection pointless.

Then, discern signal and discard noise. Not all data will be rich enough for extraction of relevant information at the cost you're willing to pay, but be careful not to disregard information-rich outliers. In many cases, it's the extreme measurements that tell the interesting story.

Draw Conclusions Reliably

The data at hand isn't always what we expect it to be. You might wish to have gotten a different result than what it really was. It is important to learn and recognize that feeling when it arises. Do not indulge it, just accept the reality—the system as perceived is not the system as found.

System engineers can develop a strong sense of intuition about system's operation. It's a useful thing to have, but the process takes time and nothing compares to strong evidence. Use your gut feeling only when looking for concrete answers is unfeasible.

That is not to say that making assumptions is inappropriate—most of the time it's necessary as it will help you save a lot of precious time. However, the more data points to support the assumption, the more reliable it will be.

Monitor Extensively

Make the monitoring platform your sharpest tool. Collect metrics from all components of your application stack, ranging from network to user experience.

Make sure you're able to drill down from highest level metrics right down to those of finest granularity. Correlate them and develop a sense of which two timeseries belong on a plot together. Be fluent in reading them—see the picture beyond the timeseries plot. Know what type of metric you're dealing with and how it was measured.

Every time you're hit by an outage, take a snapshot of the system's metrics and analyze them offline. Were early indicators present? Did some components behave unexpectedly? How did they recover?

Alarm Selectively

Alarm only on things that matter. It only makes sense to send alerts for actionable events. While any suspicious behavior should be monitored, not all of it is worth the distraction. If too much noise is generated, you'll learn too fast to ignore it. I have seen enough cases where a production issue was downplayed without further investigation based on previous experience with false positives.

Make your alerting configurations breathe the data. Where possible, set adjustable monitor thresholds to raise precision and recall of detectability and save yourself a ton of maintenance work. Reevaluate them automatically and as often as necessary. Set severities accordingly—blowing small issues out of proportion affects ability to prioritize under pressure in a bad way.

Work Smart, Not Hard

In operations, time is a scarce and precious resource. That's one of the reasons why keeping attention only on things that matter is key. Here are a few ideas to maintain a strong operational focus and make it an enjoyable task.

Learn from the Experience of Others

Organizations of different size and scale share their findings in research papers. Reuse their efforts! There is no need to learn everything from your own mistakes anymore. The Internet is an immense and expanding body of knowledge. Relevance of information is a much bigger problem than access to it. The perfect place to start is the whitepaper "On Designing & Deploying Internet-Scale Services" by James R. Hamilton. I consider it is the single most concise guide for application designers and ops teams. It encapsulates years of relevant experience in just over twelve pages of text. I guarantee that if you read it you'll be surprised how much of it is relevant to your current situation.

Have a Tactic

During daily operations things will happen that you're unprepared for. There will be no time to think and no place to hide. With the pressure on, you might experience mental blackouts. There is no good reason not to have a troubleshooting tactic at hand, just in case.

Event response is a process of answering two fundamental questions: a) what broke? b) how to fix it? Naturally, the answer to them is made up of many smaller questions. With the right questions asked in proper order the mitigation process is much faster and makes you stay in the saddle. Here is a sample troubleshooting tactic to illustrate the idea:

1. Think timeline.

   What time exactly at has the event started? Has it occurred suddenly, or were there earlier indicatives?

2. Scope out the problem.

   What portion of the system is affected? Is there user impact?

3. Look into the audit log.

   What might have caused it? What events were happening just before and at the start of the problem?

4. Tick off emergency checklist.

- If more people take part in the recovery, have their roles been assigned?
- Is the problem external or internal? If internal, is it up- or downstream from your system?
- Should others be notified? Who?

5. Work towards problem resolution.

   While researching the problem, keep an open mind, but look at the facts.

6. Carry out corrective action.

7. Monitor for recovery.

In communication with your peers:

- Do not introduce information overhead. Resist the urge to contribute the irrelevant.
- Always back your argumentation with evidence.
- Avoid chasing red herrings.
- Use intuition only when necessary.

Run a Bank of Cases

When investigating sources of suspicious fluctuations in timeseries, keep a record of your findings and try to use it in subsequent investigations. With time, a list of usual suspects will be established and following it during investigations in order of descending likelihood of occurrence will save much time and effort.

Typically a wiki-based content management system is used for recording instructions on how to deal with tickets. Unfortunately, maintenance of articles requires effort and does not always work well in practice. The articles become outdated very quickly and are hardly ever removed, resulting in a burden of documentation.

The problem can be solved when the needs are addressed directly, and what you need is a mapping of symptoms to potential causes. It would be even better if relative probability of symptom-to-cause could be established. It can! With no effort.

Make use of reporting capabilities of your ticketing system, specifically reports on root cause assignment, as described in Chapter 7.

You can make it happen with no added operational burden, if only your organization makes a habit of the following:

- The incoming ticket's summary includes symptoms of the problem, e.g. "Website response time's p99 exceeds 3 seconds."
- The tickets resolved in the past have a suspected root cause assigned to them and an audit trail of actions points at ways to resolve the problem.

If these two conditions are met, then every time a ticket comes in, the ITS can be searched by keywords from the incoming ticket's title. This action should yield a history of similar tickets resolved in the past. When the result is grouped and sorted by the number of root cause occurrences, it gives the investigating operator a massive hint as to what the suspected origin of failure might have been. When the root cause is confirmed, the operator can reuse mitigative actions carried out by his predecessors. In short, deduplication of effort.

Enjoy the Process

Busywork takes the joy out of a job; do not let that happen. You will typically find it in established organizations with entrenched status quo. Busywork will lurk in routine tasks defined by Standard Operating Procedures (SOP) or daily checklists. It is very unfortunate that these things are easier to create for no good reason than they are to eliminate them for a valid one.

Always try to make a strong case to phase out mundane tasks that have no value. Phase them out through automation and process improvements.

Most anomalies observed during system operation might not be worth digging into. When you are about to begin an investigation, do it with the goal of getting some value from the findings. If the outcome of the investigation won't matter at all, maybe it's better to invest your attention somewhere else and fry the bigger fish.

While mitigating freshly discovered faults, try to formulate repetitive tasks as repeatable steps. In this way, the task will be ready to be automated. There really is no point in keeping processes manual. Automation is fun, drives reliability, and saves you time and money.

And finally something I only realized now, while working on this book on my own: smart people who share your passions are the single most important factor in the process of professional growth. If you're lucky enough to be surrounded by a team of such talented individuals, congratulations! Make the most of it.

Setting Up OpenTSDB

OpenTSDB is a distributed timeseries database designed to accommodate the needs of modern dynamic large-scale environments. It was built with resilience in mind and has been proven to handle extremely high data loads. OpenTSDB embodies many concepts described in this book. It implements plotting functionality and has the ability to interface with alerting solutions, such as Nagios. If you're looking to build a robust and scalable monitoring platform, OpenTSDB is the right place to start.

The Software

OpenTSDB was initially developed at StumbleUpon by Benoît Sigoure to address the issues of cost-effective, long-term metric retention and durability at an extremely large scale. OpenTSDB's most distinctive feature is its decentralized nature. The implementation rests on top of HBase, a fully distributed, nonrelational database that offers a high degree of fault-tolerance. OpenTSDB uses that to provide resilience at the same time not compromising on performance and feature richness.

The code is distributed under GNU Lesser General Public License (LGPL) version 2.1.

Architecture

Figure A-1 illustrates OpenTSDB in its operation. At the core of the solution lies the *Timeseries Daemon* (TSD), which assists the clients in storing and retrieving metrics from the HBase cluster. The two core components are loosely coupled and can be scaled independently.

Multiple instances of TSDs communicate between three actors: input sources, clients, and the datastore.

Input sources are servers with data collection agents deployed to them. The collectors gather and report hardware statistics, quantitative data extracted from application logs as well as SNMP information reported by the network devices and sensors.

The clients are system operators plotting the charts via the HTTP interface, alerting systems evaluating most recent data points for existence of alertable behavior, and automated processes that use monitoring information as input for routine tasks. TSD's UI allows for juxtaposing any combination of timeseries at arbitrary temporal granularity starting with one second. The data points may also be exported over HTTP in clear text as inputs to alerting engines and for offline analysis. Such fine granularity is unprecedented at the scale that OpenTSDB can support.

Datastore typically refers to an HBase cluster, although the open source community has reported success with using alternative NoSQL solutions. It should be noted, however, that at the time of this writing HBase is the only supported datastore.

OpenTSDB's data collection takes place by pushing data to the datastore, that is, the sources report data points to TSD instances with put operations. All put operations are independent in that the reporting servers are not assigned to specific TSDs or the other way around.

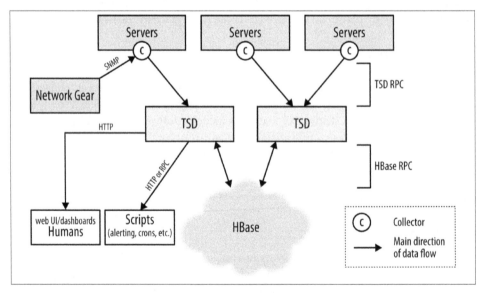

Figure A-1. OpenTSDB Architecture, courtesy of Benoît Sigoure

Getting OpenTSDB

A single-box installation of OpenTSDB can be completed in 15 minutes. It involves deploying an HBase instance and populating it with OpenTSDB schema, spinning up the Timeseries Daemon (TSD), and feeding it with data! OpenTSDB fetches most of its dependencies at build time except for GNUPlot, Java Development Kit (JDK), and HBase. These three need to be installed separately.

To bootstrap a single-node HBase instance, visit this website (*http://opentsdb.net/setuphbase.html*).

Then for the latest OpenTSDB setup instructions, go here (*http://opentsdb.net/gettingstarted.html*).

First Steps

From here on I will assume that you followed the Getting Started guide on the OpenTSDB project website and have a running instance of HBase. In particular I assume that you have completed the following:

- Downloaded and successfully built OpenTSDB
- Deployed and started an HBase instance
- Populated HBase with the OpenTSDB schema

 To verify whether you're ready to go, visit your HBase node on port 60030 (*http://localhost:60030/*) if you're running a single node cluster) and check for the existence of tsdb and tsdb-uid tables under Online Regions. If the page does not load or the tables aren't there, consult the logs in your HBase's installation *logs/* directory.

Starting TSD

Enter the *build/* directory in the root of where OpenTSDB was built. It contains the *tsdb* shellscript wrapper which you'll use for managing the TSD. Launching a TSD instance requires three mandatory command line options: the TCP port number to use, location of the web root from which to serve static files, and the request cache directory.

Addition of `--auto-metric` flag gets TSD to create metric entries in TSDB for you on the fly. Otherwise, metrics have to be created with `tsdb mkmetric` subcommand. While automatic metric creation might not be ideal for a production environment, this very convenient feature saves a lot of typing while playing with `tsdb`.

The "staticroot" should already be present in the current directory. Create the *cache* directory and start `tsdb` on port 4242.

```
$ ./tsdb tsd --port=4242 --staticroot=./staticroot --cachedir=/tmp/tsd --
auto-metric
```

The last line should read "Ready to serve". Now go here (*http://localhost:4242*). You should be greeted by TSD's HTTP interface. It's time to upload some data inputs.

Pushing Data

A running TSD instance is meant to receive inputs from data collectors in `push` mode (Figure A-2). The collectors connect to TSD and upload data via clear-text protocol with help of simple `put` operations. Submitting inputs requires four pieces of information:

Figure A-2. TSD's HTTP interface

1. The name of a metric that the input should be assigned to

2. A Unix timestamp at which to assign the value

3. The numeric value

4. One or more tags associated with the input

The template for the put directive is as follows:

```
put <metric> <timestamp> <value> <tagkey=tagvalue> [<tagkey=tagvalue> ...]
```

Every data input must to be described by at least one tag.

To report a data point simply open a TCP connection to a TSD and supply the data as follows:

```
$ echo "put test.metric $(date +%s) 1 order=first" | nc localhost 4242

$ echo "put test.metric $(date +%s) 2 order=second" | nc localhost 4242

$ echo "put test.metric $(date +%s) 3 order=third" | nc localhost 4242
```

Now, go back to the HTTP interface and in the metric form field enter "**test.metric**". An auto-suggestion helper window should pop up as you type. Leave the tags blank.

Click on the "From" field and when the calendar expands double click the "1m" link. This will set the start time at two minutes ago. Now, click on the "(now)" hyperlink next to the "To" field to select the present time as the end time of the observation. At this point, you should see a plot with three data points.

Okay, now let's report something more useful. Assuming that System Activity Reporter (SAR) is installed on your system, telling it to run with 1 second frequency should result in a fine-grained report of CPU utilization in percentage terms.

```
$ sar 1

Linux 3.0.0-22-generic (hostname) 14/07/12 _i686_ (2 CPU)

01:18:10 CPU %user %nice %system %iowait %steal %idle

01:18:11 all 18.59 0.00 13.57 2.51 0.00 65.33

01:18:12 all 19.00 0.00 13.00 0.00 0.00 68.00

01:18:13 all 20.81 0.00 11.17 0.00 0.00 68.02

01:18:14 all 17.82 0.00 12.38 0.00 0.00 69.80

...
```

The following shellscript reads in sar's output, translates it into TSDB put instructions and uploads them to TSD.

```
#!/bin/bash
# Ignore sar's header.
sar -u 1 | sed -u -e '1,3d' |
while read time cpu usr nice sys io steal idle;
do
    NOW=$(date +%s)

    echo put cpu.util $NOW $usr time=user
    echo put cpu.util $NOW $sys time=system
    echo put cpu.util $NOW $io time=io
    echo put cpu.util $NOW $idle time=idle
    # Report values to standard error.
    echo timestamp:$NOW user:$usr sys:$sys io:$io idle:$idle >&2
done | nc -w 30 localhost 4242
```

Let it run and pull up the TSD's HTTP interface in the browser:

1. Enter "cpu.util" in the metric name.

2. Select last ten minutes as start date and now as the end date.

3. The first tag field under the metric name should get populated with "time" key by now. Enter an asterisk ("*") in its corresponding value.

4. Select the "Autoreload" checkbox, and set the interval for 5 seconds.

Soon enough the resulting plot should look something like the one in Figure A-3.

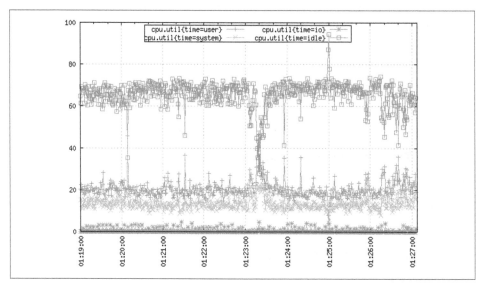

Figure A-3. Plot of SAR's CPU utilization

Input Tagging

Tagging provides an extremely convenient and flexible mechanism for aggregation by source of data at many levels. Tags are attributes of data inputs that describe their properties and origin. You can think of each tag as an added dimension on your data, with the help of which OpenTSDB will allow you to slice and dice through the data points at will.

Let me explain the idea on a simple example: network traffic measurement. On a high level, network traffic is a flow of bytes encapsulated in packets. Looking closer, each packet has a source and destination, it represents one or more of the OSI layer protocols, and it has a direction—it either leaves or enters the network. Consider monitoring traffic flow in bytes per interval of time. The put operation for each host would look something like this:

```
put traffic <time> <value> src=<hostname> subnet=<name> proto=<protocol>
direction=<in|out>
```

Reported traffic data can now be analyzed as cumulative flow, by protocol, by direction, and even by specific source host or any combination of these, for example, incoming HTTP traffic per subnet or outgoing ICMP traffic per host, as illustrated in Figure A-4.

Tag Wildcards

OpenTSDB supports basic wildcarding of tag values. This way, single metric entry may be plotted in a form of multiple timeseries, the number depending on how many tag values were reported by the sources.

There are currently two ways in which multiple timeseries can be plotted out of a single Metric tab. First, you enter the tag key in the lefthand input box next to the "Tag" label and then in the value input box

- placing an asterisk ("*") will render timeseries for all possible tag values in that metric,
- delimiting selected tag values by a pipe sign ("|") will make TSD render only the timeseries for selected tag values.

Temporal Aggregation

Short-lived technical blips that cause cascading failures up and down the solution stack happen in a matter of seconds. OpenTSDB was designed specifically to continuously monitor large clusters of servers at sufficient granularity, empowering the operators to detect and evidence problem sources without having to dig into logs just to extract quantitative information. OpenTSDB records data inputs at one second granularity, which is much finer than the vast majority of monitoring systems can offer.

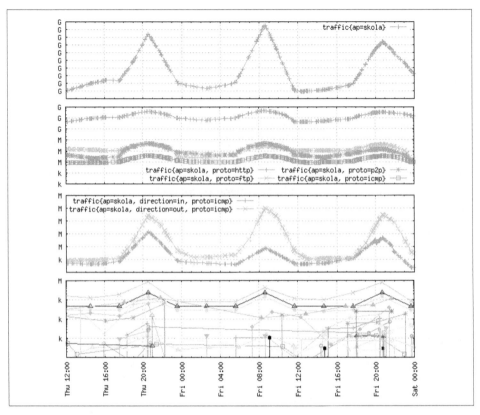

Figure A-4. 72 hours of TCP/IP traffic at different levels of aggregation

Having said that, OpenTSDB does not lock the user into data point intervals of specific length. When one second interval is too short to reliably plot the desired effect on a timeseries, it's possible to select custom temporal input aggregation. In the UI, this is referred to as *downsampling*. To make the data points on the selected metric's timeseries less granular, select the "Downsample" checkbox and enter desired interval. The TSD will divide the timeseries into an evenly spaced time period group, aggregate all data inputs reported in that duration, and summarize them with a statistic of choice.

Summary Statistics

At the time of writing this, the TSD can condense inputs into data points with a selection of summary statistics: min and max—the smallest and largest values per interval (*p0* and *p100*), the sum and average of values, and standard deviation. TSD's UI refers to summary statistics as aggregators.

Rate of Change

Rate of change is a series of data points derived from another timeseries by calculating the difference between two consecutive values from the original series.

Deriving the rate of change is especially useful for counter metrics, which are a special type of stock metric described in detail by Chapter 2. A rate of change of a counter metric is a flow-type metric, describing counter increases per interval.

For all other timeseries, rate of change illustrates the velocity of data point values: speed of their increase or decline, with the latter plotted in negative range. As a result, it usually makes sense to place the rate of change series on the right y-axis, leaving the left side y-axis for series ranging in nonnegative values only.

To plot the rate of change in OpenTSDB check the "Rate" box in the metric options window.

Gathering Data System-Wide

OpenTSDB is accompanied by a light-weight framework for data collection, *tcollector*. Its main objective is to gather inputs from local agents on all hosts in the system and push them to a TSD instance. Using tcollector over trivial, custom-built agents brings about a number of advantages:

- Occasionally crashing local collectors get restarted.
- Problems in communication with TSDs are handled for you, thus ensuring continuity of reported data.
- Repeated inputs get deduplicated to keep the overhead to the minimum.
- Data transfer to TSD is abstracted out so that any future changes to OpenTSDB will not require local code updates.

When data collection takes place from many machines system-wide, these advantages become really apparent.

The framework comes with a number of ready-made input collectors that support readouts from standard Linux interfaces and software packages, such as */proc* pseudo-filesystem, MySQL instances, and more. For custom data collection agents, *tcollector* provides a simple, clean, and consistent interface.

Running tcollector

tcollector is written in Python and comes ready-to-run with a number of standard input collectors.

To get it, check out the latest version from the official repository:

```
$ git clone git://github.com/stumbleupon/tcollector.git

$ cd tcollector
```

The directory should contain licensing files, base tcollector code and a number of standard input collectors in the *collectors/0* subdirectory. If you've started your TSD with --auto-metric option, all you need to do now is to start tcollector. The following line will kick off the process with root privileges.

```
$ sudo TSD_HOST=localhost TCOLLECTOR_PATH=. ./startstop start
```

```
Starting ./tcollector.py
```

Okay, *tcollector* is running and reporting metrics. After fifteen seconds first inputs should have arrived. Switch back to the HTTP interface and plot some metrics; for example, juxtapose proc.stat.cpu with proc.meminfo.highfree and df.1kblocks.used. A detailed description of each metric's supported by tcollector can be found here (*http://opentsdb.net/tcollector.html*).

For production settings, *tcollector* should be packaged and deployed system-wide to every monitorable host. Typical setup on each machine involves the following:

- Place *tcollector* in */usr/local/tcollector*.
- Leave only those local collectors in *collectors/0/* subdirectory that you want to gather inputs and remove all the rest.
- Place *startstop* script in */etc/init.d/tcollector* and make it start at boot time.

Writing a Custom Collector

It is extremely easy to plug a custom collection agent into tcollector—simply create an executable script or binary that reports data inputs at an interval and place it alongside other agents. The inputs should be printed one per line to standard output in similar format as for the put directive, but with the put directive itself omitted:

```
<metric> <timestamp> <value> <tagkey=value> [<tagkey=value> ...]
```

The following agent gathers temperature information for selected cities. It runs continuously in a closed loop at 5 minute intervals.

```python
#!/usr/bin/python
import sys
import time
import urllib2

COLLECTION_INTERVAL = 300
CITIES = ['Beijing', 'Cambridge', 'Farnham', 'Koeln', 'Sebastopol', 'Tokyo']
WEATHER_API = 'http://citytemp.effectivemonitoring.info/get'
```

```
def get_temperature(city, scale='c'):
    """Get temperature for a city."""
    city_url = WEATHER_API + '?city=%s&scale=%s' % (city, scale)
    api_response = urllib2.urlopen(city_url).read()
    if api_response.strip().isdigit():
        return eval(api_response)

def main():
    while True:
        for city in CITIES:
            ts = int(time.time())
            city_temp = get_temperature(city, scale='f')
            city_label = city.lower().replace(' ', '_')
            print 'temperature %d %s city=%s' % (ts,  city_temp, city_label)
        sys.stdout.flush()
        time.sleep(COLLECTION_INTERVAL)

if __name__ == "__main__":
    main()
```

tcollector will always add a host tag to the reported data. This way, data are guaranteed to have at least one dimension, and data points can always be reliably tracked back to a set of machines from which the inputs originated (Figure A-5).

Timeseries Plots

A monitoring platform should empower the operators to make the most of gathered data. OpenTSDB does exactly that. The following features make OpenTSDB's interface a powerful one:

- Setting arbitrarily many system metrics against each other to allow for visual correlation in establishing cause and effect
- Ability to model the plot on the fly through selection of summary statistic, temporal aggregation, trimming value range, rate of change and logarithmic scale transformations for each metric separately
- Browser history, allowing for multi-metric plots to be statelessly exchanged between users with a copy and paste of a URL

Plotting Tips

There exist a number of tricks that skillful plotters use to extract the desired effect. Here are just a few of them:

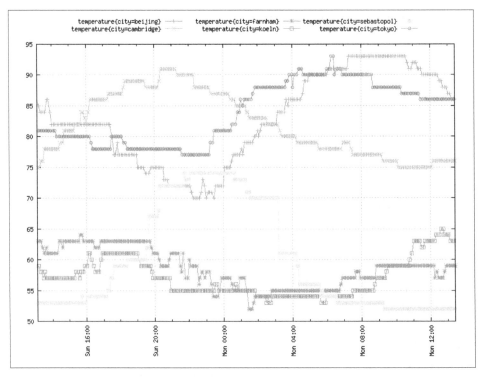

Figure A-5. Data gathered with custom collector

1. When values of data points between two timeseries differ greatly, the fluctuations described by them may become less distinct. To emphasize the deviations from baseline of both timeseries, it is best to superimpose the two by plotting them on separate scales each laid out on both left and right y-axes.

   To assign a timeseries to the right axis, check the "Right axis" box in the metric tab.

2. When three or more timeseries with data point values differing by orders of magnitude are to be plotted on a single chart, distributing the series between axes is not enough and logarithmic scale should be used. The best effect is achieved by grouping timeseries of similar magnitude on the same axes.

   Check the "Log scale" box in the Axes tab to have one of the y-axes display in logarithmic scale.

3. In view of extreme value jumps, deviations that are still significant may become obstructed. To counter this effect, the value range of the y-axes may be trimmed from top and bottom:

   Enter "[:100]" into the Range input box in the Axes window, to limit the plot from the lowest recorded value up to a value of one hundred.

4. The right balance between temporal granularity and selected time range should be struck, in accordance with what you're trying to demonstrate. Very granular graphs spanning long periods may be visually appealing, but are very hard to extract meaning from. Long data point intervals plotted over relatively short periods, on the other hand, do not convey relevant information about the process of change.

   To make default 1-second time interval coarser, click on "Downsample" and enter a selected time period, for example, 30m to plot half-hourly data points.

5. The summary statistic tells half the story. Average and median will smoothen out timeseries curves while the extreme percentiles and sum might make them spikier.

   Experiment with a summary statistic from the "Aggregator" dropdown menu of the Metric tab.

Get Involved

To learn more about OpenTSDB, visit the project's main website (*http://opentsdb.net/*). Start by reading the manual and FAQ. For the latest code changes, follow the project on GitHub (*https://github.com/OpenTSDB/opentsdb*). For current developments, join the mailing list at *opentsdb@googlegroups.com*.

About the Author

Slawek is a systems and software engineer with a background in web operations and service-oriented architectures. He specializes in implementing solutions to tough problems in large-scale information systems. Slawek has been involved in automation of infrastructures and product development, working with leading Internet giants.

Have it your way.

Milton Keynes UK
Ingram Content Group UK Ltd.
UKHW031827231123
433152UK00008B/602